T0300575

Today, most scholars agree that mismanaged monetary policy contributed to the length and severity of the Great Depression. There is little agreement, however, about the causes of the Federal Reserve's mistakes. Some argue that leadership and other organizational changes prior to the depression caused a distinct change in policy strategy that lessened the Fed's responsiveness to economic conditions. Others contend that there was no change in Fed behavior, and that errors during the depression are traceable to previous policies.

In this book, David C. Wheelock examines the policy strategy developed by the Federal Reserve during the 1920s and considers whether its continued use could explain the Fed's failure to respond vigorously to the depression. He also studies the effects on policy of the institutional changes occurring prior to the depression. While these changes enhanced the authority of officials who opposed open-market purchases and also caused some upward bias in discount rates, Wheelock concludes that monetary policy during the depression was in fact largely a continuation of the previous policy. The apparent contrast in Fed responsiveness to economic conditions between the 1920s and early 1930s resulted from the consistent use of a procyclical policy strategy that caused the Fed to respond more vigorously to minor recessions than to severe depressions.

The strategy and consistency of Federal Reserve monetary policy, 1924–1933

Studies in Monetary and Financial History

EDITORS: Michael Bordo and Forrest Capie

Barry Eichengreen, *Elusive Stability: Essays in the History of International Finance, 1919–1939*
Larry Neal, *The Rise of Financial Capitalism: International Capital Markets in the Age of Reason*
Kenneth Mouré, *Managing the franc Poincaré, 1928–1936: Economic Understanding and Political Constraint in French Monetary Policy*
Aurel Schubert, *The Credit-Anstalt Crisis of 1931*

The strategy and consistency of Federal Reserve monetary policy, 1924–1933

David C. Wheelock
University of Texas at Austin

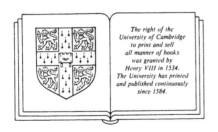

The right of the
University of Cambridge
to print and sell
all manner of books
was granted by
Henry VIII in 1534.
The University has printed
and published continuously
since 1584.

Cambridge University Press
Cambridge
New York   Port Chester   Melbourne   Sydney

CAMBRIDGE
UNIVERSITY PRESS

32 Avenue of the Americas, New York NY 10013-2473, USA

Cambridge University Press is part of the University of Cambridge.

It furthers the University's mission by disseminating knowledge in the pursuit of
education, learning and research at the highest international levels of excellence.

www.cambridge.org
Information on this title: www.cambridge.org/9780521391559

© Cambridge University Press 1991

First published 1991
First paperback edition 2004

A catalogue record for this publication is available from the British Library

Library of Congress Cataloguing in Publication data

Wheelock, David C.
    The strategy and consistency of Federal Reserve monetary policy,
1924–1933 / David C. Wheelock.
      p.   cm. – (Studies in monetary and financial history)
    Includes bibliographical references and index.
    ISBN 0 521 39155 5 hardback
    1. Board of Governors of the Federal Reserve System (U.S.)
2. Federal Reserve banks.   3. Monetary policy – United States –
History – 20th century. I. Title. II. Series.
    HG2563.W44   1991
    332.4´973´09042–dc20   91-8869
                                      CIP

ISBN 978-0-521-39155-9 Hardback
ISBN 978-0-521-53139-9 Paperback

TO MY PARENTS,
THOMAS D. AND EDRA S. WHEELOCK

Contents

List of figures

List of Tables

Preface

Many questions about the conduct of monetary policy are timeless: What should be the goals of policy? How should policy be carried out in the face of potentially conflicting objectives? How should the monetary authority be organized so as to maximize its performance? Should it be forced to follow legislated rules, or should policy makers be allowed a measure of discretion? Dissatisfaction with economic events – high inflation in the 1970s, a steep recession in the early 1980s, and financial instability throughout the 1980s – has maintained public focus on the institutions and regulations charged with managing the banking and monetary system.

This book examines the strategy and consistency of Federal Reserve ("Fed") monetary policy from 1924 to 1933. While there is now general agreement that monetary policy was mishandled during the Great Depression, there is no consensus about the causes of Fed mistakes. Were institutional factors to blame? Did leadership and other organizational changes produce a change in Fed responsiveness to economic conditions? Or did the Fed maintain a consistent policy, which became inappropriate in the face of changed circumstances? Answers to these questions would help us to better understand the role of monetary policy in the Great Depression and thus suggest how the institutions and conduct of monetary policy could be designed to avoid similar mistakes in the future.

This book is a substantial revision of my doctoral dissertation, which was completed at the University of Illinois in 1987. Many friends and colleagues have commented on portions of this work at various stages. I owe my greatest debts to my dissertation supervisor, Larry Neal, and to Michael Bordo, co-editor of this series and also a member of my dissertation committee. Their suggestions helped to focus my research and greatly enhanced its quality. A number of other individuals offered constructive criticism and suggestions for which I am grateful, including Jeremy Atack, Daniel Barbezat, Charles Calomiris, Donald Hodgman, Thomas Ferguson, Price Fishback, Subal Kumbhakar, Joseph Ritter, Raymond Sauer, Charles Swanson, Peter Temin, Steven Tomlinson, Paul Trescott, Elmus Wicker, Eugene White, and participants in research seminars at the University of California at Berkeley, University of Illinois, and University of Texas. None should be implicated for any errors in this book. I am grateful also to Academic Press Inc. for permission to draw from my paper, "The Strategy, Consistency, and Effectiveness of Federal Reserve Monetary Policy 1924–1933," in *Explorations in Economic History* 26 (October 1989, pp. 453–476), © Academic Press Inc., and to the Ohio State University Press for permission to draw from my paper, "Member Bank Borrowing and the Fed's Contractionary Monetary Policy During the Great Depression," *Journal of Money, Credit and Banking,* 22:4 (November 1990, pp. 409–426), © 1990 by the Ohio State University Press. All rights reserved. A portion of this research was funded by a Summer Research Award from the University of Texas Research Institute.

1. Introduction

The contribution of monetary forces to the Great Depression continues to be debated, but today most researchers agree that Federal Reserve System (hereinafter referred to as the "Fed") actions prolonged, if not worsened, the economic collapse. Most serious criticism of the Fed comes from monetarists such as Friedman and Schwartz (1963, pp. 300–1), who write, "The contraction is . . . a tragic testimonial to the importance of monetary forces. . . . [D]ifferent and feasible actions by the monetary authorities could have prevented the decline in the stock of money. . . . [This] would have reduced the contraction's severity and almost as certainly its duration." But many who contend that monetary forces were not paramount still argue that mistakes by the Fed contributed to the depression's severity.[1]

This study examines the causes of Federal Reserve errors during the Great Depression. Its premise is that monetary policy was mishandled and that the depression would have been less severe had the Fed taken appropriate measures to counteract it. Others have suggested a number of explanations of Fed behavior during the depression, but generally they fall into two categories. The first is that during the 1920s policy makers responded swiftly and appropriately to fluctuations in economic activity, but a change in leadership prior to the depression produced a distinct shift in Fed behavior, causing policy to be unresponsive to economic conditions thereafter. The

---

[1] Many criticize the Fed for failing to offset large outflows of bank reserves in the panic following Great Britain's abandonment of the gold standard on September 21, 1931. For example, Temin (1976, p. 170) argues that "there is evidence of monetary restriction . . . after Britain left gold in late 1931. . . . Interest rates rose in late 1931 . . . the real stock of money fell . . . [which had] depressing effects on real income." Also see Kindleberger ([1973] 1986, pp. 164–67) and Kindleberger (1988).

1

second is that there was no change in Fed behavior – the Fed's goals and methods were the same throughout, but only in the 1930s were the flaws in its policy exposed.

To better understand the causes of the Fed's failures and the role of monetary policy in the depression, further research into the strategy and consistency of Fed policy is needed. This book offers new evidence about the objectives and methods of Fed policy and examines the extent to which its failures during the depression can be attributed to flaws in a consistently used strategy or to institutional changes that altered the Fed's strategy mistakenly.

Alternative explanations of Fed policy during the depression

Testifying before the House Committee on Banking and Currency in 1935, Irving Fisher made clear his view of why monetary policy had failed to stem the Great Depression:

I myself believe very strongly that this depression was almost wholly preventable, and that it would have been prevented if [Federal Reserve Bank of New York] Governor [Benjamin] Strong had lived. . . . He discovered . . . that open-market operations would stabilize – he discovered for himself what was necessary to cure the deflation that started in May 1920 and to prevent an inflation that might otherwise come. And for 7 years he maintained a fairly steady price level in this country, and only a few of us knew what he was doing. His colleagues did not understand it. (United States House of Representatives 1935, pp. 517–520)

And Fisher argued:

The reason, or a reason why, it [the depression] was much more severe and continued into the commodity market was that Governor Strong had died and his policies died with him. . . . His successor did endeavor to . . . [continue Strong's policies] but without the degree of success of Governor Strong. I have always believed, if he had lived, we would have had a different situation. (ibid., p. 534)

Friedman and Schwartz (1963) agree with Fisher's assessment.

They stress the significance of five shocks to the financial system from 1929 to 1933 and demonstrate that the Fed responded inadequately to all but the first of them. Following the stock market crash of 1929 (the first shock), the Federal Reserve Bank of New York purchased $160 million of government securities. By the end of 1929 the Fed had purchased an additional $150 million. These purchases provided reserves that allowed the banking system to absorb stock market loans and then to liquidate them on an orderly basis. The Fed's actions contained the crisis and prevented widespread bank failures.

In contrast to its swift and effective action following the stock market crash, the Fed failed to respond decisively to other crises during the depression. It failed to supply additional reserves or currency to meet increased demands for liquidity by banks and the public during banking panics in late 1930, the spring of 1931, the fourth quarter of 1931, and in March 1933. As a result of the Fed's failure to act as lender of last resort, the money supply fell and the economy collapsed.

Friedman and Schwartz contend that under Benjamin Strong's leadership the Federal Reserve had acted to maintain macroeconomic stability but Strong's death in 1928 left a leadership void that his deputy, George Harrison, was unable to fill. Consequently, authority previously assumed by Strong was dispersed throughout the System, and the Fed's failures during the depression resulted from the "shift of power within the System and the lack of understanding and experience of the individuals to whom the power shifted" (Friedman and Schwartz 1963, p. 411). The Open Market Investment Committee, which Strong had controlled tightly, was replaced by the Open Market Policy Conference in early 1930. While just five Reserve Bank governors had served on the old committee, the Open Market Policy Conference included the governors of all twelve Reserve Banks, and the twelve "came instructed by their directors rather than ready to follow the leadership of New York as the five had been when Strong was governor" (ibid., p. 414). And, "the other Banks . . . had no background of leadership and of national responsibility. Moreover, they tended to be jealous of New York and predisposed to question what New York proposed" (ibid., p. 415).[2]

The Federal Reserve Board also had no dominant personality to promote a vigorous countercyclical monetary policy. The Federal Reserve Act gave the Board supervisory authority, but limited its power to initiate policy. The Board had rarely interfered with Strong's policies. Its only serious challenge came in 1928 and 1929 when it pressured the Reserve Banks to limit borrowing by member banks that held stock market loans, and that policy was initiated when Strong was ill and focused on international monetary reconstruction. While membership changes gradually swung the Board in favor of expansionary policies during the depression, it remained too weak to dominate policy before 1933.

The Fisher–Friedman and Schwartz view has not gone unchallenged. Wicker (1965, 1966a), Brunner and Meltzer (1968), and Temin (1989) have concluded that there was no change in Fed behavior between the Strong years and the early 1930s. In addition, other researchers have questioned whether Strong's policies actually contributed to economic stability during the 1920s.[3]

Wicker (1965, 1966a) and Temin (1989) argue that throughout the 1920s and early 1930s monetary policy reflected the Fed's commitment to the gold standard. Proponents of the gold standard believed that it was fundamental to a nation's prosperity. Even if its defense happened to be incompatible with economic stability in the short-run, as it was during the depression, the gold standard was seen as crucial for long-run stability. In the view of Wicker and Temin, the death of Benjamin Strong had little impact on policy, since he was "a passionate believer in the gold standard . . . [and] there is no evidence that he would have been more able than anyone else to break out of

---

[2] Trescott (1982) also stresses the importance of the reorganization of the Open Market Committee.

[3] Miron (1988), for example, finds that national output was less stable after the Fed's founding that it had been before, even if the Great Depression years are excluded. Toma (1989) shows that the Fed's open-market operations had no effect on the money supply during the 1920s, and Wheelock (1989) concludes that they also had little impact on total Federal Reserve credit outstanding.

the gold-standard train of thought" (Temin 1989, p. 35). Not until March 1933, when President Roosevelt devalued the dollar and began to replace conservatives on the Federal Reserve Board was there a change in monetary regime (ibid., pp. 95–98).

Of particular importance for understanding the influence of the gold standard on Fed policy are the Fed's discount rate reductions and large open-market purchases in 1924 and 1927. Friedman and Schwartz (1963, pp. 296–98, 411) argue that these actions were intended to limit recessions. But, while there were modest recessions in each year, Wicker (1966a, pp. 77–94, 110–16) concludes that the principal aim of policy was to help Great Britain retain gold by reducing U.S. interest rates relative to those in London.[4] The 1924 purchases enabled Britain to return to the gold standard at its pre-war parity in early 1925, and the 1927 purchases followed a meeting of Benjamin Strong, Montagu Norman (Governor of the Bank of England), Charles Rist (Deputy Governor of the Bank of France), and Hjalmar Schacht (President of the German Reichsbank), in which Strong apparently agreed to assist Britain through a payments crisis by lowering U.S. interest rates once again.

Friedman and Schwartz (1963) contend that the Federal Reserve's failure to respond as vigorously to the depression as it had to the recessions of 1924 and 1927 reflected a distinct change in policy regime. But Wicker (1965, p. 326) argues, "There was no dramatic shift in the quality of Federal Reserve performance. The behavior of System officials remained consistent throughout." He finds no contradiction between the Fed's actions in 1924 and 1927 and those of the 1930s:

In 1930 the international gold standard was not in imminent danger. . . . The reasons, therefore, that had been adduced in support of open-market policy by a majority of System officials both in 1924 and 1927 were simply no longer relevant. The consequence was that most Federal Reserve officials allowed their fundamental skepticism about the ability of open-market policy to moderate a business contraction to return to the surface. (ibid., p. 337)

---

[4] This view was held also by E. A. Goldenweiser (1951, pp. 141–46), Chief of the Federal Reserve Board's statistical division for much of this period. Clarke (1967) also concludes that international goals dominated Fed policy making during the 1920s.

When the goals of domestic economic stability and the gold standard came into conflict in late 1931, the Fed made its priority of defending gold clear. Great Britain left the gold standard on September 21, 1931, and speculation that the U.S. would follow resulted in a large gold outflow as foreigners converted their dollars into gold. The Fed increased its discount rate to stem the outflow, but failed to make open-market purchases to replace lost bank reserves. Despite exacerbating the depression, Fed officials determined that high interest rates were necessary to maintain convertibility of the dollar, and that open-market purchases would indicate a lack of resolve for dealing with the crisis (Wicker 1966a, pp. 163–71). While Friedman and Schwartz (1963, pp. 395–96) argue that the Fed's response to the crisis "was sharply at variance with the alternative policy the System had developed during the 1920s, the gold sterilization policy," Temin (1989) and Wicker (1965; 1966a) contend that throughout the 1920s and early 1930s the Fed was willing to subordinate domestic economic stability to the gold standard, and its behavior in 1931 reflected a continuation of its earlier policies.

Brunner and Meltzer (1968, p. 341) also argue that "a special explanation of monetary policy after 1929 is unnecessary . . . [however] an explanation based on the special attention paid to international considerations is incorrect." Brunner and Meltzer conclude that the timing of Federal Reserve operations in 1924 and 1927 indicate that international goals were not the principal motivation of policy. Rather, the Fed's mistakes in the Great Depression stemmed mainly from its continued use of a flawed policy strategy. That strategy relied on market interest rates and the level of member bank borrowing to indicate the degree of monetary ease or restraint. Because the minor recessions of 1924 and 1927 had not produced sharp declines in interest rates or bank borrowing, Fed officials inferred that money was relatively tight and consequently made substantial open-market purchases. But, because interest rates and borrowing fell to particularly low levels in the early 1930s, officials believed that money was plentiful and "cheap," and hence that specific actions to ease credit markets further were unneeded. In essence, Brunner and Meltzer contend that the Fed erred in its interpretation of monetary conditions, and that low levels of member bank borrowing and interest rates did not signal monetary ease.[5]

Epstein and Ferguson (1984) offer yet another explanation of Fed behavior during the depression. They dismiss the views that policy errors were due to changes in leadership or to a misinterpretation of monetary conditions. Rather, they contend that the Fed was deliberately contractionary in 1930 and 1931. Epstein and Ferguson argue that the Fed's objectives were to force down wages and to encourage a process of loan liquidation, which officials viewed as necessary before economic recovery could begin.[6]

The Fed seems to have had similar objectives during a recession in 1920–21.[7] Even Benjamin Strong had opposed expansionary policies in 1920, fearing they would fuel stock market speculation and interfere with necessary wage reductions. During the early 1930s many critics of the Fed argued similarly, claiming that policy had prolonged the downturn because it had created overly easy monetary conditions. And, indeed, a number of Fed officials thought that policy was "artificially" easy and argued for open-market sales to "soak-up" excess liquidity.

With the exception of Friedman and Schwartz, other researchers have traced the Fed's mistakes during the depression to the System's earlier policies. And, in arguing that institutional changes caused the Fed's failures, Friedman and Schwartz must demonstrate that the Fed had developed a strategy during the 1920s which would have been appropriate during the 1930s. Thus, to understand the reasons for Federal Reserve behavior during the depression it is necessary to study previous Fed policy actions. To what extent was System behavior during the depression a continuation of its earlier policies? That is, were the Fed's mistakes the result of a flawed strategy, maintained mistakenly in the face of changed circumstances? Or,

---

[5] Also see Meltzer (1976).

[6] Epstein and Ferguson (1984) also argue that Fed officials were influenced by the gold standard, but they emphasize the Fed's determination to force down wages, to liquidate loans, and to respond to the desires of commercial bankers.

[7] Chandler (1958, pp. 135–87) and Wicker (1966a, pp. 46–56; 1966b) analyze the Fed's objectives during this recession.

were they due to changes in the Fed's leadership and decision-making apparatus, which altered it strategy mistakenly?

Outline and methodology

This study relies primarily on quantitative analysis to address these questions. Previous researchers have worked extensively with Fed archives and the records of System officials, and have reached very different conclusions about the objectives, methods, and consistency of monetary policy. One purpose of this book is to test empirically the findings of some of these studies. The quantitative approach is thus complementary to careful historical analysis, and should not be thought of as a competing methodology. It is useful for testing alternative hypotheses, as well as to determine if policy makers acted as they claimed.

The Fed's origins and the evolution of its policy strategy following World War I are described in the remainder of this chapter. By 1924 the Fed had moved substantially away from the passive, self-regulating framework its founders had envisioned, and was attempting to manage credit markets actively with open-market operations and discount policy. The Fed's activities beginning in 1924 have received considerable attention, and much of the debate about monetary policy focuses on the System's goals and tactics from 1924 to 1933. In particular, researchers have questioned whether the Fed's policies during the depression were consistent with those from 1924 to 1929.

Chapter 2 examines the Fed's operations from 1924 to 1929. It presents reaction function estimates for each of the Fed's policy tools to test whether the Fed responded to the variables identified by Friedman and Schwartz (1963), Wicker (1965; 1966a), and other studies of Fed policy in these years. These estimates are used to forecast policy during the depression as a simple test of the consistency of the Fed's behavior over time. While the forecasts indicate that the Fed was considerably less responsive to economic conditions during the depression than it had been from 1924–29, they cannot explain *why* the Fed was less responsive.

The apparent change in Federal Reserve behavior might have

reflected a change in regime, as Friedman and Schwartz argue. Institutional changes, such as Benjamin Strong's death and reorganization of the Open Market Committee, could have altered the Fed's strategy. However, it is possible that the observed change in responsiveness in fact reflected the consistent application of a single policy strategy. A policy strategy consists not only of the ultimate goals of policy, but also the tactics used to achieve those goals. Suppose, for example, that full employment output is the ultimate goal of policy. The Fed might use open-market operations to "target" a market interest rate if it believes doing so will bring about that goal. During a recession the Fed conducts open-market operations, and thereby provides bank reserves, as needed to achieve the interest rate target that officials deem necessary to stimulate economic activity. The volume of operations needed to achieve a specific interest-rate target need not be constant over time, however, nor would the observed relationship between the level of output and open-market operations. During the depression, market interest rates fell to exceptionally low levels, despite a lack of significant open-market purchases. Fed officials believed the low interest rates reflected extreme monetary ease, and many argued that open-market purchases were unwarranted because the proximate goal of such operations – monetary ease – already existed. Although they made few open-market purchases, officials believed that they were being quite responsive to the depression. Clearly, to determine whether the apparent change in Fed behavior between the 1920s and early 1930s was in fact real, it is first necessary to study the specific strategy the System employed to achieve its ultimate goals.[8]

Chapter 3 analyzes the Fed's operating strategy and considers the

---

[8] This might suggest that reaction functions like those presented in Chapter 2 have little value in describing policy. I argue that for relatively short, economically stable periods, as from 1924–29, the relationship between the Fed's ultimate goals and its policy tools will be reasonably stable and reaction functions can help to identify the Fed's policy intent. During the interwar period the Open Market Committee determined the specific quantity of securities to buy and sell, and while it watched closely the behavior of member bank borrowing and interest rates, it did not have specific targets for these variables. Thus it seems appropriate to use the Fed's tools as the dependent variables in policy reaction functions for this period. Further discussion of how to identify the Fed's intent can be found in Chapter 2 and in Wheelock (1989).

extent to which it was used consistently from 1924 to 1933. Fed officials believed that open-market operations worked through their impact on member-bank borrowing. By altering the level of bank borrowing, officials hoped to influence market interest rates and, ultimately, their final goals. Member-bank borrowing and interest rates served as policy "indicators," that is, as variables that officials used to judge the degree of monetary ease or restraint.[9] When borrowing was low, as in 1930 and the first nine months of 1931, Fed officials inferred that money was easy, and hence that large open-market purchases were unnecessary. Econometric analysis of the demand for member-bank borrowing illustrates the flaws in the Fed's understanding of bank borrowing, and shows that its use as a policy guide during the depression permitted contraction of the money supply.

Chapter 4 considers the impact of institutional change on Federal Reserve policy during the depression. Did these changes alter Fed strategy, as Friedman and Schwartz argue? During the depression the Federal Reserve Bank of New York often advocated more vigorous policies than were accepted by the rest of the System, and undoubtedly the Fed would have been somewhat more expansionary had New York retained the level of influence it had during Benjamin Strong's tenure. But the extent to which the institutional changes altered Fed behavior fundamentally is not clear, and Chapter 4 explores some of the ways in which these changes affected policy during the depression.

The origins of the Federal Reserve System

The Federal Reserve System was designed to correct perceived flaws in the National Banking system, especially the tendency for recurrent financial crises. The Panic of 1907 led to passage of the Aldrich-Vreeland Act of 1908, which permitted banks to form associations to issue emergency currency during liquidity crises. It also created the

---

[9] The difference between an "indicator" and an "intermediate target" is that the Fed uses its policy tools to achieve a specific value of the latter, but does not for the former.

National Monetary Commission to make a detailed study of the banking system and to make recommendations for its reform.

The Commission reported its findings in 1912. It concluded that financial crises were the result of "inelasticity" in the supply of currency and bank credit. Crises were often touched off by the failure of an important financial institution, such as that of the Knickerbocker Trust Company in 1907, precipitating bank runs as the public feared for the safety of its deposits. The problem of inelasticity arose when the public attempted to convert bank deposits into currency. With fractional-reserve banking, deposits far exceed the total stock of currency, and under the National Banking system there was no formal mechanism to add to the supply of currency during a panic. The currency stock consisted mainly of national bank notes, supplemented by Greenbacks and silver certificates. The volume of national bank notes was tied to bank holdings of U.S. Government bonds, and unless the quantity of bonds outstanding changed, there was little flexibility in the supply of notes.[10]

Reformers proposed a system in which the stock of money rose and fell with agricultural and business activity. The basis of that system was the Real Bills Doctrine. To provide flexibility in the supply of credit the Federal Reserve Banks were established to rediscount short-term, self-liquidating, commercial notes for member banks. When the demand for commercial loans was high, banks could increase their lending capacity by rediscounting with the Federal Reserve. When loan demand fell, rediscounts would decline. Similarly, in the face of heavy deposit withdrawals, member banks could obtain additional currency, in the form of Federal Reserve notes, by rediscounting. By limiting the types of loans eligible for rediscount, the Fed's founders hoped to maintain a sufficient supply of bank credit to accommodate the needs of trade, as well as to

[10] Some flexibility was provided by the issue of clearinghouse certificates by various clearinghouse associations. See Timberlake (1984) and Gorton (1985) for analysis of clearinghouse activities. In addition, Treasury Secretary Leslie Shaw discovered how to influence the money supply through purchases of government bonds and by the transfer of government deposits between the subtreasuries and commercial banks (Timberlake 1978, pp. 175–85).

provide additional currency to meet emergency demands, without promoting financial speculation or inflation.[11]

Although the operations of the Federal Reserve System were based on the Real Bills Doctrine, the gold standard remained the foundation of the monetary system: "Indeed, the early Federal Reserve system, operating on a real bills principle . . . was to be a self-regulating appendage to a more fundamental self-regulating system, the operational gold standard" (Timberlake 1978, p. 222).[12] The gold standard served as both an objective of and a constraint on policy. It was seen as fundamental to general economic prosperity, as well as a check on the tendency of governments to exploit inflation, and the Fed was required to maintain a gold reserve equal to a percentage of its deposit and note liabilities. Although a clause in the Federal Reserve Act permitted emergency suspensions of this requirement, it was taken as a binding constraint and was used to justify later policy actions.

The discount rate was intended to be the principal policy tool of each Federal Reserve Bank. Although the Federal Reserve Act gave no explicit instructions on how the rate was to be set, it was assumed that the Reserve Banks would follow the gold standard "rules of the game." In the face of a gold outflow, the Banks would increase their discount rates to put sufficient upward pressure on market rates to stop the outflow. Similarly, discount rates were to be lowered in response to gold inflows.

The Reserve Banks also were authorized to make open-market

---

[11] The Reserve Banks were authorized to rediscount commercial, agricultural, and industrial paper, bankers acceptances used to finance foreign trade, and United States Government securities with maturities of up to three months. Consistent with the Real Bills Doctrine, loans used to support purely financial activity, such as stock market call loans, were excluded. In 1916 eligibility requirements were broadened to include acceptances arising from domestic trade, and the Reserve Banks were authorized to lend directly to member banks on their own notes, secured by eligible paper. See Board of Governors of the Federal Reserve System (1943, pp. 325–26) for a summary of the types of paper eligible for rediscount and for the significant changes in eligibility rules from 1914 to 1933. And see Friedman and Schwartz (1963, pp. 168–73), West (1977) and Timberlake (1978, 186–206) for analyses of the various reform proposals and more discussion of the problem of money supply inelasticity.

[12] Also see Friedman and Schwartz (1963, 189–96).

operations, both in bankers acceptances and in government securities. Initially, the sole justification for operations in government securities was to permit the Banks to obtain earning assets. The Real Bills Doctrine implied that rediscounts alone would provide sufficient liquidity to accommodate commerce and to meet financial emergencies. No discretionary operations, such as the purchase of securities, were necessary.

The Reserve Banks initiated government security operations and determined the volume they wished to buy or sell. However they did not initiate transactions in bankers acceptances. Instead, each Reserve Bank set a buying rate schedule (different rates for different maturities) and purchased all eligible acceptances offered by banks and bill dealers. There was no established acceptance market in the United States prior to the founding of the Federal Reserve System, and the Fed's founders promoted such a market for a variety of reasons:

> Among these were a desire to emulate practices in the highly developed money markets of Europe, to channel short-term open-market credit into financing of "legitimate business" and away from stock market speculation, and to enhance the regional mobility of credit, tapping the areas of plentiful credit to finance crop movements and other short-term transactions in the interior. (Chandler 1958, p. 87)

By ensuring a liquid market, acceptance operations encouraged commerce and promoted the United States' role in the world economy, objectives consistent with both the Real Bills Doctrine and the worldwide gold standard.

The Federal Reserve System had been in existence less than three years when the U.S. entered World War I. The international gold standard was suspended, and the Fed became heavily involved in financing the war. Open-market operations in government securities and discount loans secured by government securities came to dominate the Fed's activities. After the war the Fed developed new methods which emphasized the use open-market operations in government securities to manage credit markets. By 1924 new institutions, such as the Open Market Investment Committee, were in place, and the Fed had put into operation an activist policy strategy quite distinct from the passive, self-regulating framework the Fed's founders had envisioned.

The development of a policy strategy, 1914–1923

An amendment to the Federal Reserve Act in 1916 authorized the Reserve Banks to advance reserves to member banks against their holdings of government securities (or other eligible paper). During World War I the Fed offered a preferential discount rate on these loans, and between April 1917 (when the U.S. entered the war) and December 1918 member bank borrowing increased from $34 million to $1766 million (Board of Governors of the Federal Reserve System 1943, p. 373). While the Fed did not purchase large quantities of government securities during the war, it made it profitable for member banks to do so by providing reserves inexpensively. Moreover, since much of these reserves were supplied against government securities, they represented a clear departure from the Real Bills Doctrine principle.

Following the war the Federal Reserve maintained its low discount rate to enable the Treasury to complete its financing. But gold outflows and heavy borrowing by member banks reduced the Fed's reserve ratio to where it constrained System policy. The Fed was required to maintain a 40% gold reserve against its note issue and a 35% gold reserve against deposits. From a post-war peak of 50.6% in June 1919, the System's reserve ratio fell to a low of 40.6% in March 1920.[13] To discourage member bank borrowing and to raise interest rates in order to attract gold from abroad, the Federal Reserve Bank of New York increased its discount rate from 4% to 4.75% in November 1919, to 6% in January 1920 and to 7% in June 1920.[14]

Although the principal objective of the discount rate increases of 1919 and 1920 was to protect the System's reserves, the Fed also

---

[13] This is a combination of the ratios of total reserves to deposits and to Federal Reserve notes of all the Reserve Banks (Board of Governors of the Federal Reserve System 1943, p. 346).

[14] In general the other Banks followed New York's lead. Differences in the discount rates of the various Reserve Banks are analyzed in Chapter 4.

sought to control inflation and to limit stock market speculation (Wicker 1966a, p. 37–45). Nevertheless, the high interest rate policy was maintained even after inflation had been eliminated and real economic activity had begun to decline. Industrial production peaked in January 1920 and wholesale prices followed six months later, and both series fell sharply thereafter. Yet the Fed did not reduce its discount rate until May 1921 when officials were confident they could maintain the System's reserve ratio (Chandler 1958, p. 186).[15]

The Federal Reserve was harshly criticized for its actions during the immediate post-war years. In 1922 a Joint Commission of Agricultural Inquiry was appointed by Congress to investigate agricultural problems. A principal concern was whether Fed policy had contributed to falling commodity prices and high borrowing costs incurred by farmers. Although Benjamin Strong defended the System against charges that it had conspired to cause the deflation, the episode demonstrated discontent with the Fed's behavior during the violent inflation–deflation cycle of 1918–21.[16]

Perhaps in part a response to the criticism, there appears to have been a significant change in Federal Reserve behavior after 1921. This change is particularly evident in the System's use of open-market operations in government securities. From November 1921 to May 1922 the Reserve Banks individually purchased large quantities of government securities. Although made simply to augment their earnings, the purchases were followed closely by a significant easing of credit markets. The yield on short-term Treasury notes and certificates, for example, fell from 4.83% in December 1921 to 3.21% in April 1922 (Board of Governors of the Federal Reserve System 1943, p. 460). The abrupt decline in yields prompted the Treasury to complain that the Fed's operations had made it difficult

---

[15] The reserve ratio had risen to 56.4% in May 1921. Friedman and Schwartz (1963, pp. 237–38) contend that the Fed's reserve ratio was "inadequate justification" for the discount rate hikes in 1919 and 1920 since the Reserve Board had the legal right to suspend the reserve requirements temporarily. Wicker (1966b) argues that Fed officials believed that some deflation and reduction in member-bank borrowing was necessary, which was the main reason why the Fed did not reduce its discount rate sooner.

[16] See Chandler (1958, pp. 177–81) for further analysis of this episode.

to price new issues and to request that future open-market operations be coordinated with them.[17] The Federal Reserve Banks agreed to avoid future conflicts with the Treasury, and a Governors Committee was established to execute open-market operations for the Reserve Banks at the Federal Reserve Bank of New York. This committee was replaced in April 1923 by the Open Market Investment Committee, a creation of the Federal Reserve Board to better coordinate open-market operations as well as to extend the Board's control over them. A Special System Investment Account was established at the Federal Reserve Bank of New York in December 1923 to handle the committee's operations.

Beyond the adoption of new procedures, it is generally agreed that there was significant development in the use of open-market policy between 1921 and 1924. Chandler (1958, p. 234) describes this evolution:

Federal Reserve open-market operations had reached a high level of development by 1925. It had been a tortuous process with numerous errors and much friction. Nevertheless, in a period of only about three years, Federal Reserve officials had come to understand open-market operations, to develop economically meaningful objectives for them, to centralize control of them, and to use them with force and skill.

Chandler also contends that there was a parallel evolution in Benjamin Strong's understanding of monetary policy. Comparing Strong's views during the recessions of 1921 and 1924, he writes:

Like most other Federal Reserve officials, [in 1921] he believed that some deflation of bank credit was essential and that some price reductions were inevitable and desirable. Within three years, Strong himself had rejected many of these ideas. A much smaller business recession in 1924 led him to advocate large and aggressive open-market purchases of government securities and reductions of discount rates to combat deflation at home as well as to encourage foreign lending. (ibid., p. 181)[18]

Friedman and Schwartz (1963, p. 251) agree that there was significant development of monetary policy between 1921 and 1924,

---

[17] See Chandler (1958, pp. 209–32) for more detail.

[18] West (1977, pp. 195–98) argues similarly.

and highlight the contrasting descriptions of policy in the *Annual Reports* of the Federal Reserve Board for 1921 and for 1923:

> The discussion in the *Tenth Annual Report* (for 1923) is on an altogether different intellectual level. The discussion of Federal Reserve actions during the year provided the occasion for raising general issues about open market operations, their role in general policy, and their relation to discounting. . . . This was the first explicit recognition of the coordinate importance of open market operations and rediscounting for general credit policy.

And Wicker (1966a, p. 64) emphasizes that "In the *Report* [for 1923] the Federal Reserve Board extended its responsibility for monetary and credit policy to include not only the 'quality' of credit but also its 'quantity' as well." In other words, the Fed had replaced the passive Real Bills framework with a strategy involving active Federal Reserve management of the quantity of credit outstanding.[19]

By the end of 1923 the new open-market operating procedures were in place and Benjamin Strong had returned to the Fed following an extended illness. In early 1924 the Fed embarked on a new program of significant open-market purchases. Chandler (1958, p. 233) writes that "within two months of the Governors Conference in November, 1923, the Federal Reserve had resumed its purchases in government securities. . . . This time the Federal Reserve knew what it was doing, and its purchases were not for earnings but for broad policy purposes." Chapter 2 seeks to identify the "broad policy purposes" of Federal Reserve policy from 1924 to 1929, and to determine whether the Fed's responsiveness to economic conditions changed significantly between this period and the depression.

---

[19] West (1977, pp. 173–204) also reaches this conclusion.

2. The objectives of monetary policy, 1924–1933

> On the monetary side, the most notable feature [of the 1920s] was the
> close connection in timing between the movements in economic activity
> and the explicit policy measures taken by the Federal Reserve System.
>
> Friedman and Schwartz (1963, p. 296)

Friedman and Schwartz (1963, ch. 6) refer to the period 1921 to 1929
as the "High Tide of the Reserve System." Under Benjamin Strong's
leadership the Fed pursued an apparently successful policy of limiting fluctuations in economic activity, which, they argue, if continued
would have prevented a minor recession from becoming the Great
Depression.

In contrast, Wicker (1965; 1966a) contends that the apparent responsiveness of the Fed to economic fluctuations during the 1920s
was unintentional. He argues that Fed officials were concerned primarily with international goals, and that domestic economic stability
was at most a secondary objective. This view differs sharply from
that of Friedman and Schwartz (1963, p. 269), who write that "the
System frequently cited foreign considerations as a justification for
the general credit policies pursued. We are inclined, however . . . [to
conclude] that foreign considerations were seldom important in determining the policies followed."

Chandler (1958, p. 199) argues that both domestic and international goals were important:

By 1924 Federal Reserve officials had developed three major objectives or
considerations that were to shape their policies for about a decade. These
were: 1) promotion of high and stable levels of business activity and employment and stability of price levels, 2) curbing excessive use of credit for
stock market speculation, and 3) assistance to monetary reconstruction and
stability abroad.

Federal Reserve policy, 1924–1929

Prior to 1924 the Fed relied primarily on the discount rate to achieve its goals. Thereafter open-market operations in government securities played a more significant role, and usually preceded changes in the discount and acceptance ("bill") buying rates. Benjamin Strong's testimony before the House Banking Committee in 1926 suggested a shift in emphasis: "Unfortunately, it has always seemed to me that the country has given exaggerated importance to change of the discount rate, sentimentally" (United States House of Representatives 1926, p. 307). Nevertheless, Strong made clear that both open-market operations and the discount rate were integral parts of the System's strategy:

The influence that the reserve system exercises in the money market may be described . . . in this way: If speculation arises, prices are rising, and possibly other considerations move the reserve banks to tighten up a bit on the use of their credit, . . . it is a more effective program, we find by actual experience, to begin to sell our Government securities. It lays the foundation for an advance in our discount rate. . . . If the reverse conditions appear . . . as we thought were developing late in 1923, then the purchase of securities eases the money market and permits the reduction of our discount rate. (ibid., pp. 332–33)

The Fed found that discount rate changes were more effective, and yet less disruptive to credit markets, if they were preceded by open-market operations. In a letter to Montagu Norman in 1924, Strong wrote, "The effect of changes in the discount rate is more like a sledgehammer blow to sentiment, while the effect of our transactions in the open market in the purchase and sale of bills and government obligations is much gentler" (Quoted in Chandler 1958, p. 241). And he testified:

It seems to me that the foundation for rate changes can be more safely and better laid by these preliminary operations in the open market than would be possible otherwise, and the effect is less dramatic and less alarming . . . than if we just make advances and reductions in our discount rate. (United States House of Representatives 1926, p. 333)

Typically the Fed coordinated its open-market operations and discount and bill buying rate changes as Strong described. That is, open-market purchases were made in conjunction with discount and bill buying rate reductions, and sales were coordinated with rate increases. For this reason, most empirical studies of Federal Reserve policy making have focused solely on the use of one tool, usually open-market operations.[1] There were occasions, however, as in August 1929, when the Fed attempted to achieve different goals by applying its tools independently. On that occasion the Federal Reserve Bank of New York increased its discount rate and lowered its acceptance buying rate in an attempt to limit member bank borrowing and stem the flow of credit to the stock market, while simultaneously ensuring an ample supply of credit for agriculture and other "legitimate" uses.[2]

The actions taken in August 1929 illustrate the Fed's continual attempts to channel Federal Reserve credit to particular uses. Although the Federal Reserve Bank of New York argued throughout the 1920s that is was not possible to control the use of credit extended, some System officials remained convinced otherwise. A number believed that the use of reserves supplied by an open-market purchase depended upon the type of paper purchased, for example, and that the Fed had less control over the reserves supplied by a purchase of government securities than by a purchase of acceptances.[3] During the depression there were occasions when the Fed considered buying government securities, but opted instead for reducing its bill-buying rates, preferring to extend credit by purchasing real bills, rather than by purchasing government securities.[4] Thus, to understand Fed be-

---

[1] See Trescott (1982) and Epstein and Ferguson (1984), for example.

[2] See Chandler (1971, pp. 71–76) for elaboration.

[3] Friedman and Schwartz (1963, p. 266) cite a diary entry by Charles Hamlin, a Federal Reserve Board member, which illustrates the point: "there was a fundamental difference between putting money into circulation by a) Buying government securities and b) Bills; . . . [M]oney put out for b) went primarily to aid a genuine business transaction, while in the case of a) no one could tell where it might go, e.g., to be loaned on Wall Street, etc." See Wicker (1966a, pp. 127–28) for further evidence.

[4] For example, at its April 29, 1931 meeting, the Open Market Committee approved the purchase of government securities, but determined that policy should be implemented "first, through [lower] bill rates, second, through the reduction of discount rates, and then, if necessary, to resort to the purchase of government securities" (Quoted by Chandler 1971, p. 156).

havior fully it is necessary to analyze its use of each policy tool, as is done in the following three sections.

Open-market policy, 1924–1929

Today the Open Market Committee does not determine the quantity of securities to buy or sell. Rather, it adopts certain target levels for money-supply growth, bank reserves, or other variables, and directs the System's Trading Desk to carry out open-market operations as necessary to achieve those targets. To model the Fed's intent one would use the Committee's intermediate target as the dependent variable in a policy reaction function. Prior to World War II, however, the Open Market Committee itself determined the volume of open-market operations, and rarely established specific quantity targets for other variables. Thus, for these years it seems appropriate to analyze the Fed's intent by focusing on the volume of open-market operations as well as discount and acceptance buying-rate changes.[5]

This section models econometrically the Federal Reserve's open-market policy from 1924 to 1929. Specifically, the monthly change in the Fed's government security holdings (ΔGS) is regressed on measures of the various policy goals identified by Chandler (1958), Friedman and Schwartz (1963), and Wicker (1966a). To test the Fed's response to domestic economic activity, I include changes in the System's Index of Industrial Production (ΔAIP),[6] the All Commodities Price Index (ΔPRI), and a Standard and Poor's index of stock prices (ΔSTK) as explanatory variables. To capture data compilation and decisions lags, monthly changes in each index are averaged over the three months prior to the Fed's open-market opera-

---

[5] As discussed below, a limitation of this approach is that it fails to capture the Fed's use of policy indicators.

[6] The Index of Industrial Production was first available in 1927, and then constructed back in time. Thus the Fed did not have access to this index when policy decisions were made prior to 1927. However, the index is a composite of several indices which were available to policy makers. Nevertheless, the index can only be considered a proxy for the various economic data which may have influenced Fed officials.

tions.[7] The coefficient on each is expected to be negative, indicating that the Fed attempted to limit fluctuations in output, commodity prices, and stock prices. For example, to smooth fluctuations in economic activity the Fed would have purchased securities when output declined.

Wicker contends that the principal reason for open-market purchases in 1924 and 1927 was to influence the flow of gold between the United States and Great Britain. Specifically, purchases were intended to reduce U.S. interest rates relative to those in England in order to encourage the flow of gold to London. But even in 1925–26 and 1928–29 when international objectives probably were not paramount, Wicker argues they were not discarded altogether. For example, when the Fed pursued restrictive policies in 1928–29, mainly to control stock market speculation, "the [Open Market] committee was . . . not unmindful of the international consequences of rising open market rates in the U.S. *vis à vis* Europe" (Wicker 1966a, p. 131).

To test Wicker's hypothesis, I include the lagged three-month average bankers acceptance interest rates in New York (IUS) and London (IUK) as additional explanatory variables. The difference between the two rates ($IUS - IUK$) is included in an alternative specification.[8] The coefficient on the New York rate is expected to be positive, indicating that the Fed sought to stabilize rates by, for example, buying securities when domestic interest rates rose. The coefficient on the London rate is expected to be negative. And the coefficient on the differential is expected to be positive, indicating that the Fed bought government securities as the U.S. rate rose relative to that in England.

The lagged, three-month average net gold inflow (ΔG) is included

---

[7] For example, for the January 1924 ΔGS observation, the observations of the exogenous variables are the average monthly changes in each index from September to November 1923. There was a lag of about one month in the Fed's compilation of economic data. Pre-tests suggested that the fit of the model was maximized by incorporating lags of up to three months.

[8] The two rates were highly correlated. For January 1924–September 1929 the correlation coefficient between the rates is 0.55, statistically significant at the .01 level.

as an independent variable in one specification. From 1923–29 gold flows were offset by changes in Federal Reserve credit outstanding, and so they had no effect on bank reserves or the supply of money (Friedman and Schwartz 1963, pp. 279–87).[9] However, the Fed did not view gold sterilization as incompatible with its assistance to Great Britain. A gold inflow, for example, tended to reduce member-bank borrowing. But total banking system reserves changed little, if at all, since one source of reserves (gold) had simply replaced another (Federal Reserve credit). The Fed believed, however, that the reduction in member-bank borrowing would lead to a decline in market interest rates and discourage further gold inflows. Open-market purchases could reinforce this process, and Wicker argues that open-market purchases were made in response to gold inflows in 1924 and 1927 to reduce member-bank borrowing and interest rates sharply. If the Fed behaved in this manner, the coefficient on gold flows should be positive, reflecting, for example, open-market purchases in response to gold inflows.

Miron (1986) has recently argued that the Fed used open-market operations to limit the effects of seasonal fluctuations in credit demand. And Friedman and Schwartz (1963, pp. 292–96) show that changes in Federal Reserve credit offset the largely seasonal flows of currency into and out of the banking system.[10] I include the lagged three-month average change in the currency stock (ΔC) as well as seasonal dummy variables to test the Fed's response to seasonal factors. If the Fed used open-market operations to limit the effects of

[9] Federal Reserve credit is a source of bank reserves. It is the sum of the Fed's holdings of government securities, its holdings of bankers acceptances, and its discount loans (plus a small component comprised mainly of float). The monetary gold stock also is a source of reserves. Wheelock (1989) provides econometric evidence that changes in Federal Reserve credit outstanding offset gold flows during the 1920s. Gold inflows, for example, caused Federal Reserve credit to decline. Changes in member-bank borrowing and in the Fed's acceptance holdings, rather than open-market operations in government securities, accounted for most of the offsetting changes in Federal Reserve credit.

[10] Currency held by the public is a use of bank reserves. That is, as currency is withdrawn from banks, bank reserves decline. As with gold flows, changes in member-bank borrowing and in acceptance sales to the Fed account for much of the change in Federal Reserve credit offsetting currency flows. See Wheelock (1990a) for further analysis of the Fed's accommodation of seasonal credit demand.

currency flows on bank reserves, the coefficient on this variable should be positive, reflecting open-market purchases as currency held by the public rose.

Banking panics precipitated monetary collapse during the depression, and the Fed's failure to act as lender of last resort was a major policy mistake. Friedman and Schwartz are especially critical of Fed officials for this failure, and argue that the System's founders and early leaders, most notably Benjamin Strong, would have responded differently.

There were no banking panics during the 1920s, although there were relatively many bank failures. From 1924 to 1929 there were 4195 bank suspensions, an average of 699 per year (Board of Governors of the Federal Reserve System 1943, p. 283).[11] It is unclear whether the Fed reacted to these failures in any way, although among his justifications for open-market purchases in 1924, Benjamin Strong listed the "pressure on the banking situation in the West and Northwest and the resulting failures and disasters" (United States House of Representatives 1926, p. 336). But Friedman and Schwartz (1963, pp. 269–70) conclude that the Fed was largely apathetic toward bank failures, particularly since member banks accounted for relatively few failures, and the Fed felt little responsibility for non-member institutions.[12]

From its inception the Federal Reserve sought to entice banks to join the Federal Reserve System.[13] Benjamin Strong argued in 1915 that "no reform of our banking methods in this country will be complete and satisfactory to the country until it includes all banks . . . in one comprehensive system" (Quoted in Chandler 1958,

---

[11] By contrast, from 1930 to 1932, there were 5096 suspensions, an average of 1699 per year. In 1933 there were 4000 suspensions, most occurring during a banking panic, and subsequent Bank Holiday, in March.

[12] Of the suspensions from 1924–1929, 740 were Federal Reserve member banks, an average of 123 per year. Of the suspensions from 1930–1932, 1035 were member banks, an average of 345 per year (Board of Governors of the Federal Reserve System 1943, p. 283).

[13] See White (1983, pp. 127–87) for an analysis of the determinants of membership in the Federal Reserve System and of Fed attempts to encourage banks to join the System.

p. 80). Thus it seems plausible that the Fed responded differently to the failures of member banks than to nonmember banks, and so I include the lagged, three-month average change in all bank suspensions ($\Delta Fail$) and of member bank suspensions only ($\Delta MemFail$) as alternative independent variables in the open-market policy model. If the Fed responded to failures of member institutions only, the latter variable would better indicate the Fed's response. The coefficients should be positive if the Fed attempted to ease credit by buying securities in response to increases in failures. If the Fed responded to member failures only, it is conceivable that the coefficient on $\Delta MemFail$ could be positive and significant, while that on $\Delta Fail$ would not be significantly different from zero.

In their study of the Federal Reserve's open-market purchase program of 1932, Epstein and Ferguson (1984) argue that System officials believed that occasional recessions were necessary to maintain the vitality of the economy. Central to this doctrine was the notion that real wage rates had to decline before recovery could begin, and Epstein and Ferguson conclude that during the depression the Fed delayed expansionary open-market purchases until this had occurred. The Fed's restrictive policies during the 1921 recession seem also to have resulted in part from a goal of reducing wage rates (Wicker 1966a, p. 55). I include the three-month average change in the industrial real-wage rate ($\Delta Wage$), lagged one month, as a final independent variable in the open-market policy model to test whether the Fed reacted to real wages from 1924 to 1929. The Epstein–Ferguson hypothesis implies that its coefficient should be negative, i.e., that the Fed bought securities as the real wage rate fell.

Estimates of the open-market policy model for January 1924–September 1929 are presented in Table 2.1. This period omits the possibly anomalous open-market purchases following the stock market crash in October 1929. Equation 1.1 in Table 2.1 supports the hypotheses that the Fed used open-market operations to attempt to limit fluctuations in output and stock prices. Since the Durbin–Watson (DW) statistic indicates the possibility of serially correlated errors, I reestimated the model with maximum likelihood and an $AR(1)$

Table 2.1

Open-Market Policy Reaction Functions
January 1924-September 1929. Dependent variable: ΔGS

Variable	Eq. 1.1	Eq. 1.2	Eq. 1.3	Eq. 1.4
Intercept	30.75	32.70	−10.17	−20.33
	(35.57)	(43.42)	(15.31)	(24.55)
ΔAIP_{-1}	−8.30	−6.66	−7.40	−10.04
	(2.90)***	(3.41)**	(3.33)**	(2.74)***
ΔPRI_{-1}	−3.95	−3.80	−1.61	4.04
	(6.78)	(7.78)	(7.59)	(6.76)
ΔSTK_{-1}	−3.59	−3.38	−4.24	−2.84
	(1.96)**	(2.20)*	(2.05)**	(1.68)**
IUS_{-1}	21.86	21.77		
	(6.91)***	(8.63)***		
IUK_{-1}	−32.58	−33.34		
	(9.59)***	(12.11)***		
$(IUS - IUK)_{-1}$			24.26	
			(8.48)***	
ΔG_{-1}				0.59
				(0.15)***
ΔC_{-1}				0.00
				(0.33)
$\Delta Fail_{-1}$				
ρ		−0.25	−0.26	
		(0.14)*	(0.14)*	
Adj. R^2	.46	.48	.48	.48
DW	1.55	2.02	2.04	1.60
Observations	69	69	69	69

Notes: Each regression included seasonal dummy variables. Equations 1.1 and 1.4 were estimated using ordinary least squares. Equations 1.2 and 1.3 were estimated using maximum likelihood. Standard errors are in parentheses. Adj. R^2 is the R^2 adjusted for degrees of freedom.

***, **, and * indicate statistical significance at the .01, .05, and .10 levels.

Table 2.1, cont.

Variable	Eq. 1.5	Eq. 1.6	Eq. 1.7	Eq. 1.8	Eq. 1.9
Intercept	37.66 (46.32)	44.59 (41.13)	37.57 (46.15)	45.95 (41.17)	27.20 (35.74)
ΔAIP_{-1}	−6.76 (3.50)**	−8.37 (2.76)***	−6.75 (3.53)**	−8.15 (2.81)***	−7.91 (2.93)***
ΔPRI_{-1}	−4.07 (8.02)	3.72 (6.93)	−3.95 (8.04)	4.21 (7.03)	−6.52 (7.24)
ΔSTK_{-1}	−3.35 (2.29)*	−3.41 (1.88)**	−3.41 (2.27)*	−3.45 (1.87)**	−3.47 (1.96)**
IUS_{-1}	22.33 (9.14)***	16.79 (7.29)**	22.54 (9.08)***	16.94 (7.26)**	22.25 (6.92)***
IUK_{-1}	−34.79 (12.93)***	−26.92 (9.80)***	−34.64 (12.83)***	−26.89 (9.76)***	−33.11 (9.61)***
ΔG_{-1}		0.49 (0.15)***		0.49 (0.15)***	
ΔC_{-1}		−0.18 (0.33)		−0.19 (0.33)	
$\Delta Fail_{-1}$	0.09 (0.49)	−0.13 (0.43)			
$\Delta MemFail_{-1}$			0.03 (1.87)	−0.83 (1.69)	
$\Delta Wage_{-1}$					−11.90 (11.81)
ρ	−0.25 (0.15)*		−0.25 (0.15)*		
Adj. R^2	.47	.53	.47	.53	.46
DW	2.02	1.81	2.02	1.81	1.53
Obs.	69	69	69	69	69

Notes: Each regression included seasonal dummy variables. Equations 1.5 and 1.7 were estimated using maximum likelihood. Equations 1.6, 1.8, and 1.9 were estimated using ordinary least squares. Standard errors are in parentheses. Adj. R^2 is the R^2 adjusted for degrees of freedom.

***, **, and * indicate statistical significance at the .01, .05, and .10 levels.

error process (Equation 1.2). Although the coefficients on *AIP* and *STK* are somewhat smaller than in Equation 1.1, they still offer support for the hypotheses.

The coefficients on the lagged New York and London interest rates also have the anticipated signs and are statistically significant. Increases in the U.S. rate apparently led to open-market purchases, while increases in the U.K. rate led to sales. Equation 1.3 includes the rate differential as an independent variable, and its coefficient also has the expected sign and is statistically significant. Equation 1.4 includes lagged gold flows as an explanatory variable. Its coefficient is consistent with Fed purchases to reinforce the impact of gold inflows on bank reserves, therefore offering further support of Wicker's hypothesis.

The coefficient on currency flows is not statistically significant. However, this probably does not imply that the Fed was unconcerned with such flows. Rather, because currency flows were largely seasonal this variable is highly collinear with the set of seasonal dummy variables. Moreover, currency flows were offset mainly through changes in member-bank borrowing and in the volume of acceptances sold to the Reserve Banks.

The coefficients on all bank failures ($\Delta Fail$) and on member bank failures only ($\Delta MemFail$) are also not statistically significant (Equations 1.5–1.8). It appears the Fed's attitude toward failures was indeed one of apathy. George Harrison, who became Governor of the Federal Reserve Bank of New York following Benjamin Strong's death, testified in 1931 about the number of bank failures during the 1920s:

It was due, in part, I think to the changed economic set-up in the whole country; due to the fact that, with the automobile and improved roads, the smaller banks . . . with nominal capital, out in the small rural communities, no longer had any reason really to exist. Their depositors welcomed the opportunity to get into their automobiles and go to the large centers where they could put their money. (United States Senate 1931, p. 44)

Like Harrison, most Fed officials believed that bank failures were a normal consequence of changing economic conditions. Unfortunately, the Fed was slow to recognize the economic differences between the relatively harmless failures of the 1920s and the sweeping panics of the depression.[14]

Finally, Equation 1.9 includes the change in the industrial real-wage rate as an explanatory variable. Although its coefficient has the anticipated sign, it is not statistically different from zero. The hypothesis that the Fed responded to changes in the real-wage rate is not supported by the data for 1924–29.[15]

The open-market policy regressions indicate clearly the Fed's attempts to limit fluctuations in economic activity, to control stock market speculation, and to assist Great Britain retain gold. Did the Fed use its discount and acceptance buying rates compatibly with open-market operations? Or, did it attempt to achieve different goals with its different tools? The following sections analyze the Fed's rate policies from 1924 to 1929 to obtain a more complete picture of System behavior in these years.

Discount rate policy, 1924–1929

In testimony before Congress in 1926, Benjamin Strong outlined the factors which led the Federal Reserve Bank of New York to change its discount rate:

The rates of discount are fixed after considering almost every element that enters into the credit situation, including consideration of the rates of interest in the market, the course of prices . . . to some extent, whether there is much speculation or inventories are piling up or not, whether the flow of business is uniform, and even somewhat with relation to the foreign movement of gold. (United States House of Representatives 1926, p. 329)

The policy goals identified in the various histories of the Federal Reserve System are consistent with Strong's list. Thus, I include

---

[14] In addition to Friedman and Schwartz (1963), Temin (1976; 1989), Wicker (1980; 1982), Bernanke (1983), and White (1984) research the nature and significance of bank failures during the depression. More recent research by Calomiris (1990) and Alston, Grove and Wheelock (1991) has sought to explain bank failures during the 1920s.

[15] $\Delta Wage$ was included in some of the other specifications as well. In none was its coefficient significant, and the coefficients and significance levels of the other variables were not substantially affected.

again changes in the production (ΔAIP), commodity price (ΔPRI), and stock price (ΔSTK) indices as independent variables in the discount-rate model. The sign of each coefficient is expected to be positive, indicating that the Fed increased its discount rate in response to increases in each index, and lowered it when each index fell. For example, if the Fed sought to limit fluctuations in output it would reduce the discount rate when output was falling in order to encourage bank borrowing and credit expansion.

The change in the U.S. monetary gold stock (ΔG) and the New York–London interest rate differential ($IUS - IUK$) are also included again as independent variables to test the Fed's response to international monetary conditions. The coefficient on changes in the gold stock is expected to be negative, reflecting, for example, discount rate reductions in response to gold inflows for the purpose of lowering domestic interest rates and repelling further inflows. Similarly, the coefficient on the New York–London rate differential should be negative, reflecting, for example, discount rate reductions in response to increases in the New York rate relative to that in London. Such action would be designed to encourage borrowing and lower domestic interest rates. Finally, the two measures of bank failures ($\Delta Fail$ and $\Delta MemFail$), and the change in the real-wage rate ($\Delta Wage$) are included again as independent variables. The coefficients on $\Delta Fail$ and $\Delta MemFail$ should be negative if the Fed sought to ease credit in response to increases in failures, while that on $\Delta Wage$ should be positive if the Fed reduced its discount rate as real wages fell. Note that all of the anticipated signs are consistent with those expected in the open-market policy model, i.e., that open-market purchases (sales) coincided with discount rate reductions (increases).

The economic cost of borrowing from the Federal Reserve is the difference between the discount rate and the cost of acquiring reserves from an alternative source, such as by selling a security.[16] Thus, if market interest rates rise relative to the discount rate, the economic cost of borrowing from the Fed declines. The Fed did

---

[16] This abstracts from other possible costs of borrowing, such as increased Fed surveillance a bank incurs when it borrows. A model of member bank borrowing is presented in Chapter 3.

not adjust the discount rate continuously to match changes in market rates, but Benjamin Strong implied that the discount rate was changed when it was deemed too far out of line with market rates.[17] To capture this adjustment, I include the difference between the discount rate and the market rate on short-term bankers acceptances $(DR - IUS)$, lagged one period, as an additional independent variable. Its coefficient is expected to be negative, indicating that the discount rate was reduced as the discount rate–market rate differential rose, all else unchanged.

Figures 2.1 and 2.2 plot the discount rate of the Federal Reserve Bank of New York and monthly changes in that rate from January 1924–February 1933, respectively. The discount rate was changed just twelve times between January 1924 and September 1929, and always in discrete intervals, usually one-half or one point at a time. The observations in Figure 2.1 are weighted averages, where the weights are based on the number of days a particular rate was in effect during a month. The first-differences of the observations in Figure 2.1 are plotted in Figure 2.2, and I use this series as the dependent variable in the discount rate policy model (ΔDR). These adjustments introduce some additional variability into the data and hence overcome some of the econometric difficulties associated with estimating a model in which the values of the dependent variables are discrete. Nevertheless, caution must be observed in evaluating the results.[18]

Estimates of the discount rate policy model for January 1924–September 1929 are reported in Table 2.2. Equations 2.1 and 2.2 are identical except that Equation 2.1 includes the lagged average New York–London interest rate differential as an independent variable, while Equation 2.2 includes the lagged average change in the gold

---

[17] See Mayer, Duesenberry, and Aliber ([1981] 1987, p. 317) for a discussion of why the Fed does not adjust the discount rate continuously to match changes in market rates.

[18] When the observations of the dependent variable of an econometric model are discrete, ordinary least squares estimates of the model coefficients are biased and inefficient. Nevertheless, most previous studies use OLS. An alternative approach is adopted by Eichengreen, Watson, and Grossman (1985) who use a modified probit model to estimate Bank of England Rate policy reaction functions.

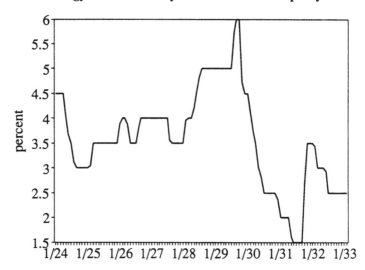

January 1924--February 1933

Figure 2.1. Discount rate: Federal Reserve Bank of New York.

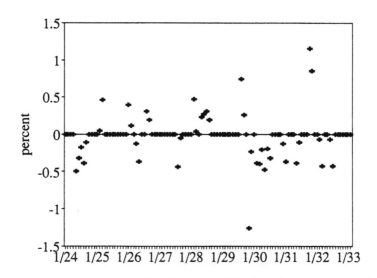

January 1924--February 1933

Figure 2.2. Monthly change in discount rate: Federal Reserve Bank of New York.

Table 2.2

Discount Rate Policy Reaction Functions
January 1924-September 1929. Dependent variable: ΔDR

Variable	Eq. 2.1	Eq. 2.2	Eq. 2.3	Eq. 2.4	Eq. 2.5
Intercept	−0.62 (3.78)	1.33 (3.20)	−1.16 (3.89)	1.06 (3.25)	2.41 (3.23)
$(DR - IUS)_{-1}$	−0.16 (0.06)***	−0.15 (0.06)***	−0.15 (0.06)***	−0.14 (0.06)***	−0.16 (0.06)***
ΔAIP_{-1}	2.18 (1.37)*	2.26 (1.30)**	2.13 (1.39)*	2.23 (1.32)**	2.43 (1.29)**
ΔPRI_{-1}	2.48 (3.03)	0.64 (2.97)	2.43 (3.06)	0.64 (3.00)	−1.02 (3.11)
ΔSTK_{-1}	2.55 (0.83)***	2.42 (0.76)***	2.55 (0.84)***	2.40 (0.77)***	2.31 (0.76)***
$(IUS - IUK)_{-1}$	−0.03 (0.03)		−0.04 (0.03)		
ΔG_{-1}		−0.18 (0.07)***		−0.18 (0.07)***	−0.18 (0.07)***
$\Delta Fail_{-1}$			0.09 (0.16)	0.09 (0.15)	
$\Delta Wage_{-1}$					−6.77 (4.23)
Adj. R^2	.32	.38	.32	.38	.40
DW	1.65	1.74	1.65	1.75	1.79
Obs.	69	69	69	69	69

Notes: ΔDR, $DR - IUS$, and $IUS - IUK$ are in basis points. Each regression was estimated using ordinary least squares. Standard errors are in parentheses. Adj. R^2 is the R^2 adjusted for degrees of freedom.

***, **, and * indicate statistical significance at the .01, .05, and .10 levels.

stock instead. The signs of all of the coefficients, except those on bank failures (Equations 2.3–2.4) and the real wage (Equation 2.5), are as expected. The results are consistent with the hypotheses that the Fed adjusted the discount rate to follow changes in market rates, to limit fluctuations in output, prices, and stock market prices, and to respond to gold flows by increasing the discount rate in response to outflows and by decreasing it in response to inflows. Finally the results suggest further that from 1924–29 the Fed did not respond to bank failures, either to those of all banks or those of member banks only, or to changes in the real-wage rate.[19] Overall, the discount rate reaction function estimates corroborate those for open-market policy, and support Chandler's (1958) view that both domestic and international goals were important determinants of Fed policy during the 1920s. And both sets of estimates indicate the Fed's general disregard for bank failures and the behavior of real-wage rates. The following section provides further evidence of the Fed's policy intent by examining the setting of its acceptance-buying rate.

Acceptance-buying rate policy, 1924–1929

The acceptance-buying rate schedule was the third policy tool available to the Federal Reserve. The Reserve Banks purchased all bills of acceptable quality and maturity offered by member banks and bill dealers at the Fed's buying rates. The Banks rarely sold any bills except under agreement to repurchase (Burgess [1927] 1946, pp. 172–73).

The founders of the Federal Reserve System sought to establish a market in bankers acceptances in the United States similar to that in London. Their goal was to promote the dollar as an international currency, and especially to encourage the financing in the United States of U.S. exports and imports. By January 1925 there were $835 million of dollar-denominated acceptances outstanding, an amount comparable to the amount of commercial paper outstanding. The volume of acceptances continued to increase, both absolutely and relative to the volume of commercial paper outstanding. At its interwar-period peak in December 1929, acceptances outstanding totaled $1732 million, while commercial paper totaled just $334 million (Board of Governors of the Federal Reserve System 1943, pp. 465–66).

---

[19] Re-estimating Equations 2.3–2.4 in Table 2.2 using $\Delta MemFail$ in place of $\Delta Fail$ as an independent variable produces coefficient estimates (standard errors) of 0.20 (0.30) and 0.36 (0.29). Neither is statistically significant, and none of the coefficient estimates or significance levels of the other independent variables is substantially affected.

The growth of the American acceptance market was encouraged by the Fed's willingness to purchase bills, and the Reserve Banks held a large share of outstanding acceptances during the 1920s. The System's holdings peaked in December 1919 at $574 million, and the Fed's holdings were never less than $100 million before mid-1929. During the depression the Fed's holdings fell, however, and by mid-1934 it held less than $1 million of bills (ibid., pp. 465–66).

Typically, bill-buying rates were adjusted to follow changes in market rates. According to Burgess ([1927] 1946, p. 234), "the fixing of the rate for buying bills is less a matter of policy than the fixing of the discount rate for loans. The buying rate for bills ordinarily follows closely changes in the open market rates for bills." Nevertheless, the bill-buying rates were also adjusted along with the discount rate and with open-market operations in government securities to achieve a variety of policy objectives.

Figure 2.3 plots the buying rate of the Federal Reserve Bank of New York on 61–90 day bills, along with that Bank's discount rate from January 1924–February 1933. Except in August 1929, the rates

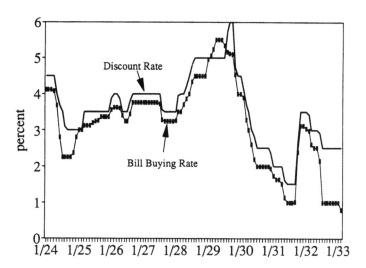

January 1924--February 1933

Figure 2.3. Bill-buying and discount rates: Federal Reserve Bank of New York.

were always changed in the same direction. Thus, it seems likely that the variables which can explain discount rate adjustments also can account for changes in the bill-buying rate. I model the first-difference of the rate (ΔBR), and include all of the variables used to explain changes in the discount rate as independent variables in the bill-buying rate regressions. The difference between the Fed's buying rate and the market rate on acceptances of like maturity ($BR - IUS$), lagged one period, also is included as an independent variable. Its coefficient is expected to be negative, indicating that the Fed increased its buying rate when the market rate rose relative to the Fed's rate, and lowered it when the market rate fell, all else unchanged.

Acceptance-buying rate model estimates for January 1924–September 1929 are presented in Table 2.3. The results support the hypothesis that the Fed kept the bill-buying rate in line with market rates. They suggest also that the Fed responded to fluctuations in output and stock market prices, and to changes in the monetary gold stock. Increases in output or stock prices led to increases in the Fed's buying rates, while gold inflows were followed with reductions in the buying rates. These results are entirely consistent with those for open-market policy and discount-rate changes reported above.[20]

Federal Reserve policy, 1929–1933

Was Federal Reserve policy during the depression consistent with, or predictable from the System's actions during the 1920s? As a simple test of the consistency of Federal Reserve policy over time, I forecast Fed actions during the depression from the various regression estimates for 1924–29.[21] The forecasts from several of the regressions

[20] Re-estimating Equations 3.3–3.4 in Table 2.3 using $\Delta MemFail$ in place of $\Delta Fail$ as an independent variable produces coefficient estimates (standard errors) of 0.04 (0.26) and 0.07 (0.27). Neither is statistically significant and none of the coefficient estimates or significance levels of the other independent variables is substantially affected.

[21] A more rigorous method of evaluating the consistency of policy would be to employ statistical analysis to test the stability of the reaction functions over time. Such tests can identify both whether there was statistically significant coefficient variation and when those changes occurred. Wheelock (1987, ch. 2) presents such an analysis for models like those of this chapter. In general the results support the inferences drawn from the forecasts presented here.

Table 2.3

Bill Buying Rate Policy Reaction Functions
January 1924-September 1929. Dependent variable: ΔBR

Variable	Eq. 3.1	Eq. 3.2	Eq. 3.3	Eq. 3.4	Eq. 3.5
Intercept	-4.88	-1.37	-5.62	-1.63	-1.75
	(2.93)	(2.28)	(3.07)	(2.34)	(2.33)
$(BR - IUS)_{-1}$	-0.75	-0.68	-0.74	-0.68	-0.68
	(0.16)•••	(0.17)•••	(0.16)•••	(0.17)•••	(0.17)•••
ΔAIP_{-1}	3.45	3.78	3.62	3.92	3.66
	(1.20)•••	(1.21)•••	(1.22)•••	(1.24)•••	(1.22)•••
ΔPRI_{-1}	-0.87	-1.25	-0.82	-1.17	-0.42
	(2.63)	(2.69)	(2.66)	(2.73)	(2.86)
ΔSTK_{-1}	1.73	1.42	1.81	1.45	1.47
	(0.72)•••	(0.69)••	(0.73)•••	(0.70)••	(0.70)•••
$(IUS - IUK)_{-1}$	-0.06		-0.06		
	(0.03)••		(0.03)••		
ΔG_{-1}		-0.13		-0.13	-0.13
		(0.07)••		(0.07)••	(0.07)••
$\Delta Fail_{-1}$			-0.08	-0.07	
			(0.14)	(0.14)	
$\Delta Wage_{-1}$					3.36
					(3.88)
Adj. R^2	.52	.52	.52	.51	.52
DW	1.62	1.63	1.65	1.65	1.66
Obs.	69	69	69	69	69

Notes: ΔBR, $BR - IUS$, and $IUS - IUK$ are in basis points. Each regression was estimated using ordinary least squares. Standard errors are in parentheses. Adj. R^2 is the R^2 adjusted for degrees of freedom.

•••, ••, and • indicate statistical significance at the .01, .05, and .10 levels.

and the actual levels of the Fed's policy tools are plotted in Figures 2.4–2.6. Figure 2.4 plots forecast levels of the Fed's government security holdings based on Equations 1.1 and 1.4 from Table 2.1. The difference between the forecast holdings and the Fed's actual holdings in a particular month is the cumulative forecast error from September 1929 to that date. While the forecast security holdings from the two models differ somewhat, in each case from mid-1930

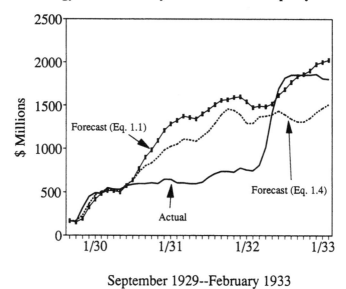

September 1929--February 1933

Figure 2.4. Federal Reserve Government Security holdings: actual and forecast.

until early 1932 they are substantially higher than the Fed's actual security holdings.[22]

Immediately following the stock market crash the Federal Reserve Bank of New York purchased $160 million of government securities, and by the end of 1929 the Reserve System had purchased an additional $150 million. The lack of a general banking panic and modest recovery in the stock market in early 1930 suggested to most observers that the crisis had been contained and that the recession would be limited.[23]

The recession was, however, not limited. The decline in economic activity that had begun in mid-1929 accelerated following the stock market crash, and continued to decline until mid-1932.[24] The Fed

[22] Forecasts based on the other models from Table 2.1 are similar.

[23] See Temin (1976, pp. 76–78) for a compilation of contemporary forecasts.

[24] The Fed's Index of Industrial Production (seasonally adjusted) peaked at 125 in June 1929 (1923–25 = 100). In January 1930, July 1930 and January 1931 the index stood at 106, 93, and 83. The index reached its low at 58 in July 1932 (Federal Reserve Board, *Annual Report*, 1937, pp. 173–77).

made a few open-market purchases in 1930 and 1931, and System holdings of government securities rose from $485 million in January 1930 to $736 million in September 1931. But, relative to the decline in economic activity, the purchases were small compared with those made during the recessions of 1924 and 1927 (see Table 2.4).

The Fed also did little to offset the effects of banking panics accompanying the economic collapse. "The general tenor of System comments [about bank failures] ... was defensive, stressing that bank failures were a problem of bad management which was not the System's responsibility" (Friedman and Schwartz 1963, p. 358). Most officials failed to comprehend the significance of banking panics, as distinct from the failure of individual insolvent firms. The fact that most of the banks failing during panics in 1930 and the first half

Table 2.4

Fed Policy During Three Recessions

Date	AIP	GS	DR
Jul 1929	124	147	5.0
Oct 1929	118	154	6.0
Jan 1930	106	485	4.5
Apr 1930	104	530	3.5
Jul 1930	93	583	2.5
Oct 1930	88	602	2.5
Jan 1931	83	647	2.0
Apr 1931	88	600	2.0
Jul 1931	82	674	1.5
Oct 1931	73	733	3.5
Apr 1923	106	229	4.5
Jul 1923	104	97	4.5
Oct 1923	99	91	4.5
Jan 1924	100	118	4.5
Apr 1924	95	274	4.5
Jul 1924	84	467	3.5
Oct 1924	95	585	3.0
Jan 1925	105	464	3.0
Oct 1926	111	306	4.0
Jan 1927	107	310	4.0
Apr 1927	108	341	4.0
Jul 1927	106	381	4.0
Oct 1927	102	506	3.5
Jan 1928	107	512	3.5

Notes: AIP is Index of Industrial Production (seasonally adjusted); GS is the Federal Reserve's government security holdings (in $ millions); DR is the discount rate of the Federal Reserve Bank of New York (in %).

of 1931 were small, rural nonmember institutions undoubtedly contributed to the Fed's inaction.[25]

A particularly severe crisis followed Great Britain's abandonment of the gold standard in late September 1931. Speculation that the U.S. would also leave gold led foreigners to withdraw deposits from American banks, causing a $500 million decline in the monetary gold stock by the end of October. Panic withdrawals of currency accounted for a further $500 million outflow of reserves between the end of September and January 1932. The Fed responded to the crisis by increasing its discount and bill-buying rates in an attempt to stem gold outflows. It purchased only $50 million of government securities during the crisis, however, not nearly enough to offset the reserve losses suffered by banks. Despite the higher discount and bill-buying rates, member banks did increase their discount window borrowing and sold over $400 million of acceptances to the Reserve Banks. Yet, total member-bank reserves fell from $2333 million in September 1931 to $1907 million in February 1932 (Board of Governors of the Federal Reserve System 1943, p. 371).

The Federal Reserve justified its failure to purchase enough securities to offset the outflows of gold and currency by claiming that it lacked sufficient gold reserves to increase its liabilities through open-market purchases (Federal Reserve Board *Annual Report,* 1932, pp. 16–19). Friedman and Schwartz (1963, pp. 399–406) and Wicker (1966a, pp. 169–71) dispute this, however, but Epstein and Ferguson (1984, pp. 964–65) argue that Fed officials did feel constrained by a lack of gold reserves. Wicker (1966a, pp. 196–70) suggests that policy makers believed that open-market purchases would further weaken confidence in the Fed's resolve to deal with the crisis. The Fed remained committed to the gold standard it had worked to restore

---

[25] Not all of the failures fit this description. A notable exception was the failure of the Bank of United States, a large New York City member bank, in December 1930. Friedman and Schwartz (1963, pp. 308–13) attach considerable importance to this failure, arguing that it was solvent and should have been saved to prevent further panic and decline in the supply of money. However, Wicker (1982) and Lucia (1985) conclude that this failure was not as significant as Friedman and Schwartz contend, and Lucia argues also that the Bank of United States was hopelessly insolvent and should not have been saved.

during the 1920s. There appears to have been no serious discussion of suspending the Fed's gold reserve requirement, even though the Federal Reserve Act allowed suspension in an emergency. Rather, the Fed acted much as it had in 1919–20 when it increased the discount rate in order to stem a decline in its reserve ratio, and kept its rate high despite a contraction in economic activity.

Whatever the reason for the Fed's failure to purchase a large quantity of securities during the crisis, the Glass–Steagall Act of 1932 largely removed the gold reserve constraint by permitting the Reserve Banks to use government securities as collateral for their note issues. The Fed began a $1 billion open-market purchase program in March 1932. Friedman and Schwartz (1963, p. 322) contend the Fed was reluctant to purchase securities but was compelled by Congress to do so. Epstein and Ferguson (1984, pp. 966–67) agree, but argue also that major banks wanted the Fed to support bond prices. Although these purchases were far larger than any previous operation, they did little but replace the reserves lost during the 1931 crisis.

Figures 2.5 and 2.6 plot forecasts of the discount and bill-buying rates of the Federal Reserve Bank of New York from October 1929–February 1933, based on regression estimates for January 1924–September 1929.[26] It appears that the New York Fed reduced its rates about as rapidly in 1930 as forecast. By mid-1931 the forecast levels of the discount and buying rates turn negative because of the accumulation of rate reductions predicted by the first-difference models. Since the rates cannot be negative, the forecasts are not meaningful for the later years, and I have constrained them to zero. Moreover, the events in late 1931, which induced the Fed to raise its rates, were unique, and could not be predicted from econometric analysis of System policy from 1924–29.[27]

In addition to Federal Reserve government security holdings and

---

[26] The forecast values of the discount rate are based on Equation 2.1 in Table 2.2, and forecast values of the bill buying rate are based on Equation 3.1 in Table 2.3. The other regressions yield similar forecasts.

[27] That is, there was no occasion between 1924 and 1929 when the Fed's gold reserves fell to a point where the System's reserve requirement constrained policy.

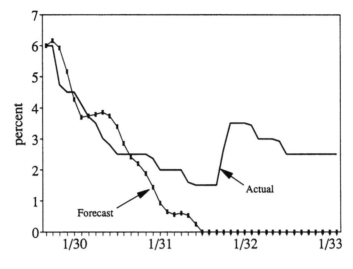

September 1929--February 1933

Figure 2.5. Federal Reserve Bank of New York discount rate: actual and forecast.

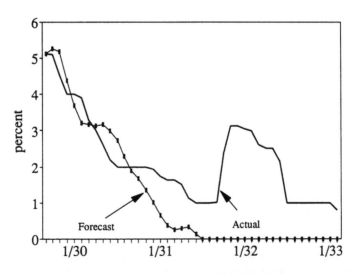

September 1929--February 1933

Figure 2.6. Federal Reserve Bank of New York bill-buying rate: actual and forecast.

the Index of Industrial Production, Table 2.4 compares the level of the New York Reserve Bank's discount rate during the recessions of 1924, 1927, and 1929–31. Unlike open-market policy, it does seem that relative to the decline in economic activity the Fed's discount rate reductions in 1930–31 were similar to those in 1924 and 1927. On the surface, this suggests support for the Friedman and Schwartz explanation of "inept" Federal Reserve policy during the depression. The shift in authority away from the Federal Reserve Bank of New York to the other Reserve Banks and Federal Reserve Board could account for the apparent lack of open-market policy responsiveness after 1929, but general consistency of the Federal Reserve Bank of New York's rate policy. New York lost much of its influence over the former tool but retained considerable discretion over its rates.[28] This explanation is supported further by the fact that during the depression the other Reserve Banks did not reduce their rates to the extent that New York did.

There is an alternative explanation of the apparent contrast in open-market policy between the 1920s and early 1930s, however, which is consistent with the Brunner–Meltzer (1968) explanation of Fed errors. Following the stock market crash, market rates fell sharply and continued to decline until the fourth quarter of 1931. Many observers, both within and outside the Fed, believed that the low rates signaled exceptional monetary ease, and that monetary policy had been implemented fully to promote economic recovery. Because it appeared that money was already easy, open-market purchases were viewed as unnecessary. The reductions in the Federal Reserve Bank of New York's discount and bill buying rates in 1930 and 1931 were made simply to keep them in line with market rates, as had been done during the 1920s. This explanation suggests that there was no change in Federal Reserve strategy with the onset of the depression, and that

---

[28] Discount and bill-buying rate changes were initiated by the individual Reserve Banks and either approved or disapproved of by the Federal Reserve Board. There were a number of instances between 1928 and 1932 when the New York Bank proposed rate changes which were not approved, however, and thus the Bank did not have complete control over its rate policy.

the organizational changes stressed by Friedman and Schwartz had little effect on policy.[29]

The following chapters consider each of these alternative explanations of the apparent change in Fed responsiveness to economic conditions. Chapter 3 examines the strategy implemented by the Federal Reserve during the 1920s and considers the extent to which that strategy continued to guide System policy during the depression. Chapter 4 studies the effects on policy of the leadership and other organizational changes occurring within the Reserve System with the onset of the depression.

---

[29] Wicker (1966a) also argues that there was no inconsistency in Fed behavior over time, and that the Fed did not make large open-market purchases in 1930–31 because the System's international objectives did not call for such action. Wicker agrees, however, with Brunner and Meltzer's claim that the Fed did not respond vigorously to declining economic activity because officials believed that low nominal interest rates and little member-bank borrowing signaled exceptional monetary ease, and that the Fed behaved similarly during the 1920s: "We are . . . in fundamental agreement that the period between 1922 and 1933 reveals a record of fundamental consistency and harmony with no sharp breaks in either the logic or the interpretation of monetary policy. We simply differ about the significance to be attached to international considerations in explaining the consistency of the performance of the monetary authorities" (Wicker 1969, p. 319).

3. Member-bank borrowing and the Fed's policy strategy

> The influence of the reserve banks upon the volume of credit is . . . felt not directly, but indirectly through the member banks. The reserve banks do not "push" credit into use.
>
> Benjamin Strong
> (United States House of Representatives 1926, p. 468)

The Federal Reserve used its policy tools, especially open-market operations in government securities, less aggressively during the Great Depression than it had from 1924 to 1929. This change in responsiveness could have come from a fundamental change in policy strategy, perhaps resulting from the death of Benjamin Strong in 1928 and the subsequent reorganization of the Open Market Committee. Or, the Fed's actions during the depression might in fact have been consistent with the goals and methods it employed during the 1920s.

The Federal Reserve believed that it could achieve its objectives by influencing the cost and availability of bank credit. Open-market operations affected the extent of member-bank borrowing from the Fed, which System officials believed had a direct impact on market interest rates. Open-market purchases provided reserves that permitted a reduction in member-bank borrowing and led to generally easier credit conditions. Open-market sales withdrew reserves, created a reserve need which banks satisfied by increasing their borrowing, and led to higher interest rates. In general the Fed did not specify quantity targets for borrowed reserves or interest rates, but watched each closely as indicators of monetary conditions.

The Fed adopted similar tactics in 1982, when it began to use borrowed reserves as an operating target. Monetarists have criticized this procedure because it does not yield effective control of the

45

money supply (Thornton 1988). In this chapter I argue that during the 1920s and early 1930s the System's operating tactics caused monetary policy to be ineffective, even destabilizing, in that the Fed's strategy did not produce effective control of the money stock. The borrowed-reserves procedure was particularly inappropriate during the depression because of instability in borrowed reserve demand induced by financial crises. The Fed failed to account for these shifts, and continued to interpret little borrowing as a sign of exceptional monetary ease. So, despite widespread bank failures and deflation, Fed officials saw little need for vigorous open-market purchases.

The next section describes the Fed's tactics, focusing especially on its theory of borrowed-reserve demand. The following sections analyze empirically the demand for borrowed reserves during the depression, and illustrate the impacts of the decline in economic activity and the financial crises on that demand. Like Wicker (1966a) and Brunner and Meltzer (1968), I conclude that there was no significant change in Fed procedures between the 1920s and early 1930s, and that the Fed's mistakes during the depression can be attributed largely to its failure to interpret monetary conditions correctly.

The Fed's strategy and theory of member-bank borrowing

During the early 1920s the Fed observed that when it purchased government securities in the open market the volume of member-bank borrowing tended to fall by a like amount. But, despite this apparent inability to change the total volume of Federal Reserve credit outstanding, the Fed observed that market interest rates did seem to respond to its operations. The Fed inferred that "various monetary factors – such as gold movements, changes in currency demand, and open-market operations by the reserve banks . . . determine the volume of indebtedness [of member banks to the Federal Reserve]. . . . And changes in this indebtedness appear to be the initiating force in corresponding changes in money rates" (Riefler 1930, p. 27). Thus largely exogenous flows of nonborrowed reserves were seen as the principal cause of member-bank borrowing. And changes in member-bank borrowing were thought to produce changes in market interest rates. The Fed inferred that open-market purchases stimulated economic activity by reducing borrowed-reserve demand and interest rates. And, similarly, that sales increased member-bank borrowing and led to higher rates which would slow economic activity.

Fed publications and statements by System officials during the 1920s make the Fed theory of member-bank borrowing clear. The classic statement of the theory was made by Riefler (1930). According to Riefler (1930, p. 28), "member banks are in general reluctant to borrow from the reserve banks, [and] when they do borrow they are in most cases motivated by necessity rather than profit." For an individual bank, deposit outflows produce the necessity. But for the system as a whole, the need for borrowing comes from open-market sales, gold outflows, or any other reduction in nonborrowed reserves.

Although he argued that in general banks do not borrow to exploit profit opportunities, Riefler (1930, p. 34) accepted that bank decisions to borrow were influenced by the differential between the yield on short-term securities and the discount rate: "it seems highly probable that member banks when they borrow and when they adjust their operations to repay their borrowing are affected to a certain extent by its cost in relation to money rates in the market."

The notion that banks are reluctant to borrow reserves, and do so only when forced to, is fundamental to the Fed's use of borrowed reserves as a policy guide. If this theory is correct, then the level of borrowing will indicate accurately the degree of monetary ease or restraint. Relatively heavy borrowing will reflect pressure on bank reserve positions and tight money, while little borrowing will reflect monetary ease. But, if the Fed's theory is incorrect, and banks do borrow to expand their loans and investments, the level of borrowed reserves will not reflect monetary conditions accurately. Since loan demand increases during economic expansions and declines during recessions, a specific level of borrowed reserves might reflect monetary ease during an expansion and tight money during a recession. Moreover, if the Fed targets a specific level of borrowed reserves, the money supply will tend to increase during expansions and decrease during recessions. For example, during a recession member-bank borrowing tends to decline since loan demand falls. If borrowed reserves fall below the Fed's target, the Fed will be tempted to sell securities. The worse a recession, the greater the decline in borrowed reserves, and, paradoxically, the more restrictive the Fed is likely to be. The Fed actually contributes to economic instability by exacerbating procyclical swings in the supply of money.

The Fed did not have an inflexible borrowed-reserves target during the 1920s or early 1930s, and it did not sell securities during recessions. However the Fed did interpret relatively heavy borrowing by banks as a sign of tight money, and little borrowing as a sign of ease. Moreover, from the level of borrowed reserves the Fed determined the appropriate volume of open-market operations necessary to achieve its goals. Benjamin Strong made this clear in a statement to the Governors Conference in 1926:

> Should we go into a business recession while the member banks were continuing to borrow directly 500 or 600 million dollars ... we should consider taking steps to relieve some of the pressure which this borrowing induces by purchasing Government securities and thus enabling member banks to reduce their indebtedness. ... Future changes in our loan account are especially significant as a guide. ...
>
> As a guide to the timing and extent of any purchases which might appear desirable, one of our best guides would be the amount of borrowing by member banks in principal centers. ... Our experience has shown that when New York City banks are borrowing in the neighborhood of 100 million dollars or more, there is then some real pressure for reducing loans, and money rates tend to be markedly higher than the discount rate. ... When member banks are owing us about 50 million dollars or less the situation appears to be comfortable, with no marked pressure for liquidation. ... In the event of business liquidation now appearing it would seem advisable to keep the New York City banks out of debt beyond something in the neighborhood of 50 million dollars. (Quoted in Chandler 1958, pp. 239–40)

This statement suggests that Strong would have judged money to be quite easy in 1930–31, since member-bank borrowing averaged just $243 million from January 1930–September 1931 (Board of Governors of the Federal Reserve System 1943, p. 371).[1] It is not evident from Strong's statement that policy would have been more expansionary in 1930–31 had he lived. It suggests also why the Fed made relatively large open-market purchases during minor recessions in 1924 and 1927, but made few purchases in 1930–31.

The Fed's government security holdings and member bank borrowed reserves from January 1924–September 1931 are plotted in Figure 3.1. Fed security holdings and the borrowed reserves of weekly reporting banks in New York City are plotted in Figure 3.2. From March–September 1924 the Fed bought some $440 million of securities. The borrowed reserves of all member banks had averaged $620 million in the three months prior to the beginning of these purchases, and did not fall below $250 million during the purchase months. New York City banks had borrowings of just over $80 million when the Fed began to buy securities, and their borrowings fell to under $10 million by mid-year. From March–December 1927 the Fed bought $300 million of securities. The borrowings of all member banks averaged $514 million in the three months prior to March, and did not fall below $400 million during the year. New York City member banks held between $50 million and $100 million of borrowed reserves throughout the year.

With the steep economic downturn, borrowed reserves declined more substantially in 1930–31 than in 1924 or 1927. From January 1930–September 1931 the Fed bought $290 million of securities. Although borrowed reserves had reached nearly $1 billion in late October 1929, they declined sharply thereafter. Borrowing by New York City banks was especially low, and in a number of months during 1930 and 1931 these banks did not borrow at all. Consequently the Fed inferred that money was already quite easy, and that few open-market purchases were necessary. Unfortunately, the stock of money fell in 1930–31 because the Fed failed to offset the decline in bank borrowing.

---

[1] Member-bank borrowing increased sharply in the final week of September 1931 because of heavy deposit withdrawals brought on by Great Britain's break with the gold standard. The Fed did not buy securities in response, however, claiming that it lacked sufficient gold reserves to back increased liabilities (see Chapter 2).

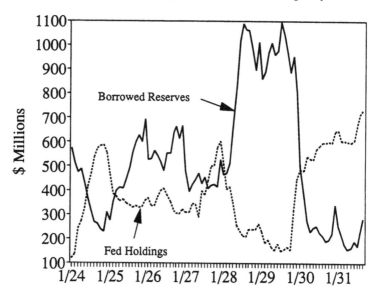

January 1924--September 1931

Figure 3.1. Member-bank borrowed reserves and Federal Reserve Government Security holdings.

Since Benjamin Strong's death is fundamental to Friedman and Schwartz' (1963) explanation of the failures of monetary policy during the depression, it is important to know precisely Strong's understanding of the transmission process and of the behavior of borrowed reserves. His statement to the Governors Conference indicates he viewed borrowed reserves as an important guide to monetary conditions. And his testimony that the "reserve banks do not 'push' credit into use" is significant since it implies a view that expansionary operations are appropriate and effective only if there is an increasing demand for Federal Reserve credit.

Strong's understanding of borrowed reserve demand is less clear. In a speech to the Harvard Graduate Economics Club in 1922 he stated:

Practically all borrowing by member banks from the Reserve Banks is *ex post facto*. The condition which gives rise to the need for borrowing had already come into existence before the application to borrow from the Reserve Bank was made, and experience has shown that large borrowings in New York City have in the past usually been explained by the member bank as caused by the borrowing operations of the Treasury, by seasonal demands, but more frequently because of the withdrawal of deposits. (Quoted in Chandler 1958, pp. 196–97)

Moreover, Strong said:

In the long run, it is my belief that the greatest influence upon the member bank in adjusting its daily position is the influence of profit or loss.... It may, therefore, be safely stated that as business expands . . . member banks will borrow from the Reserve Banks to make good deficient reserves caused by the expansion of their loans.... If borrowing at the Reserve Bank is profitable beyond a certain point, there will be strong temptation to use surplus reserves when they arise for the purpose of making additional loans rather than for repaying the Reserve Bank. (ibid., p. 196)

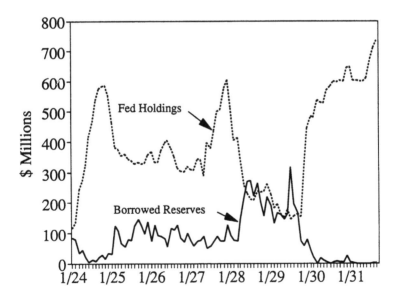

January 1924--September 1931

Figure 3.2. Member-bank borrowed reserves of New York City banks and Federal Reserve Government Security holdings.

And Strong testified before the House Banking Committee in 1926:

> When the country banks borrow of the reserve banks and continue to borrow for a long period, we generally try to find out what the occasion of the borrowing is. It may be that they are borrowing from us just to buy securities. . . . It frequently occurs that member banks who have stock exchange loans have to borrow from us for at least one day. . . . They frequently borrow for longer periods before calling their stock exchange loans. (United States House of Representatives 1926, p. 345)

Thus, while Riefler's theory recognized that the decision to borrow further or reduce outstanding discounts depends on the relative cost of doing so, it did not recognize that banks would borrow expressly to increase their earning assets. Strong seems to have made this link, however. But Brunner and Meltzer (1968) contend that Strong's view of member-bank borrowing was consistent with Riefler's.[2] A statement by Strong to the Governors Conference in 1926 supports their contention: "Experience in the past has indicated that member banks when indebted to the Federal Reserve Bank of New York . . . constantly endeavor to free themselves from the indebtedness, and as a consequence such pressure as arises is in the direction of curtailing loans" (Quoted in Chandler 1958, p. 239). Although these statements are somewhat contradictory, it does seem that Strong was aware that banks borrowed reserves to extend new loans and to pursue profitable investments. But, he also viewed member-bank borrowing as an appropriate policy guide and as central to the transmission of monetary policy to credit markets. Apparently Strong did not reject the use of borrowed reserves as a policy guide, despite the implication that if banks do borrow to extend new loans, then the level of borrowing will not reflect monetary conditions accurately.[3]

The Real Bills Doctrine, upon which the Fed's founders intended the System to operate, implies that member-bank borrowing should decline during recessions since a lower level of economic activity

---

[2] Brunner and Meltzer refer to this view as the "Riefler–Burgess Doctrine." Meltzer (1976) calls it the "Riefler–Burgess–Strong" analysis.

[3] Of course, I have had to be selective in my quotations. See Strong's testimony in United States House of Representatives (1926), Chandler (1958), Friedman and Schwartz (1963, Ch. 6), and Wicker (1966a) for more extensive evidence about Strong's views.

requires less Federal Reserve credit to sustain it. Most Fed officials believed it was appropriate that Federal Reserve credit contract during recessions. Indeed a minority argued for open-market sales to hasten the decline. Strong believed that open-market purchases should be made during recessions, but he did not advocate increases in total Federal Reserve credit outstanding.

Was the Fed's theory of the transmission process and its interpretation of member-bank borrowing during the depression consistent with that of 1924–29? An answer to this question would provide considerable evidence for the debate over policy consistency.

Wicker (1965, 1966a) and Brunner and Meltzer (1968) argue that there was no inconsistency in Fed behavior between the 1920s and early 1930s. Referring to open-market policy in 1930, Wicker (1966a, p. 156) writes, "the New York [Federal Reserve] bank did not . . . contemplate substantial purchases of government securities. Its objective was limited in scope and did not go beyond the goal set out by . . . Strong in the nineteen-twenties – that is, to eliminate the indebtedness of the New York and Chicago banks." However, Schwartz (1981, p. 42) and Epstein and Ferguson (1984, p. 961) contend that officials of the Federal Reserve Bank of New York understood that member-bank borrowing was not an appropriate policy guide, but since they do not provide direct quotes it is difficult to know precisely the views of these officials. Friedman and Schwartz (1963, p. 370) cite a July 1930 statement by George Harrison, who became Governor of the Federal Reserve Bank of New York after Strong's death, which suggests that he understood this error: "[A]n even small amount of borrowing under present conditions is as effective a restraint as substantially a greater amount was a year ago." But Wicker shows that Harrison ceased to advocate open-market purchases after member-bank borrowing by money-center banks had been eliminated. In a July 18, 1930 letter to other Reserve Bank governors, Harrison wrote:

The condition which we have desired, and for the attainment of which we believed purchases of Government securities might have been necessary, has been achieved. . . . We believe that the important end to be achieved . . . is that the money center banks should be substantially out of debt and that there should be surplus funds available. (Quoted in Wicker 1966a, pp. 156–57)

And arguing later against open-market purchases after member-bank borrowing had reached a minimum, Harrison said that further purchases would be "forced investments, and the dangers of inflation were great and the advantages doubtful" (ibid., p. 157)

Another official of the Federal Reserve Bank of New York, W. Randolph Burgess, was among the strongest proponents of open-market purchases during the depression. But in his book, Burgess ([1927] 1946, p. 250) indicated clearly that there was no change in Fed behavior between the 1920s and early 1930s:

From 1922 through 1927 the response of the economic organism to relatively small changes in Federal Reserve policy was extraordinary. But in 1928 and 1929 and later in the depression even the most vigorous measures taken by the Reserve System had relatively little effect. Member bank borrowing, interest rates, and the growth of bank credit did indeed respond in a measure but these in turn failed to influence the country's economy.

To Burgess, there was no inconsistency in the use of monetary policy, only in the economy's response to it.

Burgess (ibid., p. 54) also restated Riefler's model of member-bank borrowing: "Banks usually borrow because their reserves have become impaired; that is, they borrow after the event which makes it necessary. Only rarely do they borrow specifically to lend again. . . . " But, "there were usually some banks, however, which tended to overuse the borrowing privilege" (ibid., p. 61). His explanation of the relationship between member-bank borrowing and interest rates was again the classic Fed theory presented by Riefler:

When the member banks find themselves continuously in debt at the Reserve Banks, they take steps to pay off that indebtedness. They tend to sell securities, call loans, and restrict their purchases of commercial paper and other investments. The consequence is that when a large number of member banks are in debt, money generally becomes firmer . . . and rates increase. Conversely, when most of the member banks are out of debt . . . money rates . . . become easier. This relationship rests largely on the unwillingness of banks to remain in debt at the Reserve Banks. (ibid., pp. 220–21)

Moreover, Burgess (ibid., p. 195) argued, "interest rates are a sensitive index of changing credit conditions. They are perhaps the best available measure of the adaptation of the credit supply to the country's needs."

Chandler (1971, pp. 133–59) analyzes the policy views of several Fed officials during the depression. It is clear from his study that during the early 1930s most believed that money was exceptionally easy since market interest rates and borrowed reserves were low.[4] Federal Reserve publications, such as the *Bulletin,* indicate also that the Fed believed money was easy during 1930 and during the first eight months of 1931. For example, the October 1930 issue states: "Easy credit conditions at the present time are general throughout the county, as indicated by the small volume of indebtedness of member banks to the reserve banks in all Federal Reserve Districts" (Federal Reserve *Bulletin,* October 1930, p. 613).

The Fed's use of a free-reserves strategy in the 1950s and 1960s was an extension of the strategy developed during the 1920s, and it seems unlikely that the Fed abandoned the strategy during the depression.[5] Undoubtedly the Fed would have been more expansionary, particularly in early 1930, had the Federal Reserve Bank of New York retained its role as System leader. But it does seem that the Fed's failures during the depression were due largely to its flawed strategy. The central flaw in that strategy was the use of borrowed reserves as a policy guide. The following sections illustrate empirically the errors in the Fed model of the demand for borrowed reserves. The results demonstrate the inadequacies of the Fed's theory and suggest further the causes of monetary-policy errors during the Great Depression.

---

[4] In fact, as Chandler (1971) and Epstein and Ferguson (1984) show, some Fed officials argued that open-market purchases would have been harmful, interfering with a process of "liquidation." For example, Chicago Fed Governor James McDougal argued against purchases in 1930, claiming, "it would be inadvisable to force additional credit into an already oversupplied market." In 1931 McDougal advocated open-market sales, arguing that the Fed's policies had created artificially easy monetary conditions (Chandler 1971, p. 135).

[5] Free reserves equal excess less borrowed reserves. See Meigs (1962) for analysis of the flaws in a free reserves strategy, and Brunner and Meltzer (1964) for a discussion of the Fed's use of free reserves as a policy indicator and target during the 1950s and 1960s.

An alternative model of the demand for member-bank borrowing

The first challenge to the theory of member-bank borrowing described by Riefler was from Turner (1938). While Riefler concluded that member-bank borrowing was generally unresponsive to the discount rate, or to the difference between the discount rate and market interest rates, Turner reached the opposite conclusion, and went on to describe how banks were responsive to the alternative costs of acquiring reserves. Modern theoretical and empirical studies of member-bank borrowing, such as Goldfeld and Kane (1966), Dutkowsky (1984), and Dutkowsky and Foote (1985) derive from Turner's pioneering work.

In the Goldfeld–Kane model a bank is faced with an uncertain reserve need, perhaps due to deposit withdrawals or to the bank's own expansionary activities, which is met either by selling a short-term security or by borrowing from the Fed. The reserve need is assumed to be composed of permanent and transitory components. For the empirical analysis, the bank's expected permanent reserve need is measured as a weighted sum of current and past flows of nonborrowed reserves and the intercept, reflecting the bank's desires to expand its earning assets. Given these flows, the bank chooses between selling a security and borrowing, depending upon the spread between the yield on the security and the discount rate. Finally, lagged borrowed reserve levels are included in the model to capture stock adjustment. The Goldfeld–Kane model is thus:

$$B_t = a_0 + a_1 (I - DR)_t + \Sigma b_i \Delta R^n_{t-i} + \Sigma c_j B_{t-j} + e_t \qquad (1)$$

where B = the level of borrowed reserves
I = market interest rate
DR = Federal Reserve Discount Rate
R^n = the level of nonborrowed reserves[6]

---

[6] Goldfeld and Kane did not adjust for changes in required reserves until Aigner and Bryan (1968) noted that such an adjustment should be made. From 1924–33 there were no changes in required-reserve ratios, but because of flows between different bank classes and types of deposit accounts, there were changes in the aggregate effective required reserve ratio. Unfortunately, the data on types of deposits by bank classes do not exist before 1929 which would allow me to correct nonborrowed reserves for these changes.

Δ = first difference operator

e = random error with zero mean and constant variance.

The principal difference between this model and that of Riefler (1930) is the explicit incorporation of bank desires to expand their asset portfolios, although Goldfeld and Kane do it rather crudely. I use the Goldfeld–Kane model, but, like Goldfeld (1966), estimate the change in borrowing (ΔB), rather than the level. This equation is derived simply by subtracting B_{t-1} from each side of the Goldfeld–Kane model. Ignoring lagged changes in nonborrowed reserves and those of more than one period in the level of borrowed reserves, the basic model of the flow of borrowed reserves is thus (time subscripts suppressed):

$$\Delta B = a_0 + a_1 (I - DR) + b_0 \Delta R^n + (c_0 - 1)B_{-1} + e \qquad (2)$$

Dutkowsky (1984) and Dutkowsky and Foote (1985) extend the Goldfeld–Kane model to account for nonlinearity in the relationship between bank borrowing and the market interest rate–discount rate spread. In addition to the discount rate (and transactions costs), Dutkowsky's model incorporates bank reluctance to borrow from the Fed and Fed surveillance of borrowing banks as additional borrowing costs. These latter costs increase with the level of borrowing, and do so at an increasing rate. Dutkowsky derives a switching model of borrowing in which member bank borrowing is zero below some (positive) rate spread. At higher spreads borrowing is positive, but since the implicit cost of borrowing rises as the level of borrowing increases the relationship between borrowing and the rate spread is nonlinear. Finally, at a sufficiently high rate spread, all of the bank's reserve need will be satisfied by borrowing from the Fed and borrowing will be invariant with respect to the rate spread.

Following Dutkowsky, I incorporate switching behavior and nonlinearity in my econometric analysis of borrowed reserve demand for the 1920s and early 1930s. However, the extent to which the Fed discouraged bank borrowing varied considerably during these years, and hence the applicability of the reluctance/surveillance costs depends on the specific years studied.

During World War I and in the immediate post-war months, the Federal Reserve encouraged member banks to purchase U.S. Government obligations by offering a preferential discount rate on borrowings against these securities. Bank borrowing increased substantially in these years, from $34 million in April 1917 (when the U.S. entered the war) to a peak of $2708 million in October 1920.[7] Although the Reserve Banks initiated significant discount rate increases beginning in November 1919, the preferential rate on borrowings secured by Government securities was not eliminated by all Banks until November 1921. Thus, at least during the war and for some months after, Fed surveillance and bank reluctance to borrow probably had little, if any, effect on borrowing.

By 1920 the Fed's attitude toward member-bank borrowing had begun to change. Although the principal reason for discount rate increases in 1919 and 1920 was to limit further declines in the System's reserve position, Fed officials also hoped to control inflation and stock market speculation by curtailing discount loans (Wicker 1966a, pp. 32–45). Debate within the Fed centered on how to provide sufficient credit for Treasury financing operations and other "legitimate" needs without simultaneously encouraging the use of Fed credit for speculation (Chandler 1958, pp. 153–69).

Throughout the 1920s Fed officials became increasingly concerned with limiting the use of Federal Reserve credit to finance stock market speculation. The disagreement within the Reserve System in 1928 and 1929 about how to control this usage is well known.[8] The Federal Reserve Board called on the Reserve Banks to refuse loans to any bank carrying stock market loans. Although the Reserve Banks generally favored discount-rate hikes to limit borrowing, instead of "direct pressure," they did monitor borrowing banks closely.[9]

---

[7] For comparison, total member bank reserves equaled $712 million in April 1914 and $1817 million in October 1920 (Board of Governors of the Federal Reserve System 1943, pp. 373–74).

[8] See Friedman and Schwartz (1963, pp. 254–68) and Wicker (1966a, pp. 129–43) for analysis of this episode.

[9] In response to a Senate Banking Committee survey in 1931, most of the Reserve Banks indicated that they discouraged continuous borrowing by member banks (United States Senate 1931, pp. 790–92).

Certainly Fed surveillance was a non-negligible borrowing cost in these years, and it is appropriate to incorporate this cost in the empirical analysis of member-bank borrowing.

In contrast to the Fed's theory of member-bank borrowing described by Riefler, Goldfeld and Kane argue that banks might borrow reserves to accommodate customer loan demand.[10] During the 1920s and early 1930s the Fed observed that flows of nonborrowed reserves, generated primarily by open-market operations, gold, and currency flows, led to opposite changes in borrowed reserves. System officials inferred that the pressure on bank reserve positions generated by these flows was the principal determinant of bank borrowing. But, despite the tendency of member-bank borrowing to offset changes in nonborrowed reserves, total banking system reserves were not constant in these years. Member-bank borrowing declined during the economic downturns in 1924, 1927, and 1929–31, suggesting that as output fell and the demand for loans declined, banks borrowed less from the Federal Reserve. If not offset, total reserves and perhaps the money supply would have fallen.[11]

The substantial decline in borrowed reserves in the early 1930s was likely due in part to decreased loan demand as output and stock market activity declined. I include changes in bank debits (Debits) to capture the influence of economic activity on borrowed-reserve demand. Suitable monthly data on loan demand are unavailable for the interwar period, as are estimates of national income. Bank debits have often been used as a proxy for income; moreover, they capture financial transactions and other transfers which are sources of loan demand but are not part of current national income. It is expected that increasing debits meant greater loan demand and hence led to increased member-bank borrowing from the Federal Reserve.

---

[10] Earlier, Hodgman (1961) had argued that bank desires to accommodate customer loan demand is a principal determinant of member-bank borrowing. And Goldfeld (1966) found loan demand to be a significant explanatory variable in his member-bank borrowing regression.

[11] As noted above, it is probably extreme to argue that Fed officials were unaware of the procyclical nature of borrowed reserves. However it is clear that they did view borrowing as an appropriate policy guide and, moreover, that there was no reason to offset declines in borrowed reserves during depressions.

A second major flaw in the Fed's model was its failure to account for possible instability in borrowed-reserve demand. Friedman and Schwartz (1963, pp. 332–50) show that banking panics produced sharp declines in the deposit–reserve and deposit–currency ratios during the depression. Banks became more conservative and were probably less willing to borrow reserves. Describing the failure of borrowing to increase sufficiently to replace outflows of nonborrowed reserves in late 1931, Friedman and Schwartz (1963, pp. 318–19) write:

> The aversion to borrowing by banks, which the Reserve System had tried to strengthen during the twenties, was still greater at a time when depositors were fearful for the safety of every bank and were scrutinizing balance sheets with great care to see which banks were likely to be the next to go.

A lack of eligible paper to use as collateral for discount loans also could have contributed to a down-shift in borrowed-reserve demand during the depression. Although the total volume of eligible paper outstanding far exceeded member-bank borrowing throughout the depression, Chandler (1971, pp. 225–33) shows that this paper was not distributed evenly among member banks and argues that a lack of collateral prevented many banks from borrowing.[12]

Most Federal Reserve officials apparently believed that member banks had an adequate supply of eligible paper, particularly prior to the fourth quarter of 1931 (ibid., pp. 226–32). The Fed seems also to have been oblivious to the effects of financial crises on the willingness of banks to borrow, and continued to interpret little borrowing as a sign of extreme monetary ease. I include a dummy variable (D) set equal to 1 during the depression and to 0 before it to test the hypothesis that a downward shift occurred in the borrowed-reserve

---

[12] He argues, "This is not to say that an inadequate supply of eligible assets was solely responsible for the failure of banks to borrow more to maintain or expand their loans and investments. Also relevant were the unwillingness of some banks to show borrowings on their balance sheets or to assume the risks of borrowing and lending [and] the tendency of some, but not all, Reserve banks to be overly conservative in valuing eligible assets and in determining their acceptability" (Chandler 1971, pp. 232–33). Gendreau (1990) also argues that a tightening of Reserve Bank credit policy beginning in March 1929, coupled with a lack of eligible paper, caused a significant down-shift in member-bank borrowing during the depression.

demand function. The complete model of borrowed-reserve demand estimated here is thus:

$$\Delta B = \alpha_0 + \alpha_1(I - DR) + \alpha_2 \Delta R^n + \alpha_3 B_{-1} + \alpha_4 \Delta Debits$$
$$+ \alpha_5 D + e_1 \qquad (3)$$

where $(I - DR) \leq (I - DR)^*$

$$\Delta B = \beta_0 + \beta_1 \ln(1 + I - DR) + \beta_2 \Delta R^n + \beta_3 B_{-1} + \beta_4 \Delta Debits$$
$$+ \beta_5 D + e_2 \qquad (4)$$

where $(I - DR) > (I - DR)^*$.

The rate differential $(I - DR)^*$ is the spread at which switching occurs. When the spread is less than or equal to $(I - DR)^*$ borrowing will not be the least-cost means of acquiring reserves, and discount loans will be minimal. In this regime borrowing should not be affected by the particular level of the rate spread, or by the bank's desire to accommodate loan demand. Hence the α coefficients should equal zero. Nevertheless, because the model is estimated with aggregate data these variables are included in Equation 3. The particular differential at which switching occurs will differ across banks, so in the aggregate borrowing will likely be somewhat responsive to these variables. Equation 4 models borrowing when the rate spread is above the switchpoint. Following Dutkowsky (1984), I assume the relationship between borrowing and the rate spread is log-linear in this region.[13] The coefficients β_1 and β_4 are expected to be positive, while β_2, β_3 and β_5 are expected to be negative.

The determinants of member-bank borrowing: econometric evidence

Regression estimates of the demand for member-bank borrowing for January 1924–February 1933 are reported in Tables 3.1 and 3.2. Separate results are presented for all member banks in the New York

[13] Also like Dutkowsky (1984), I do not attempt to estimate the upper switchpoint, i.e., the spread at which banks satisfy all of their reserve needs by borrowing and the demand for borrowed reserves is completely inelastic. Dutkowsky argues that the log-linear form captures adequately the leveling out of borrowing at higher rate differentials.

Table 3.1

The Demand for Member Bank Borrowing
New York District
January 1924-February 1933. Dependent variable: ΔB

	Eq. 1.1	Eq. 1.2	Eq. 1.3
Intercept	14.40	15.93	2.24
	(6.52)**	(8.18)*	(8.82)
$(I - DR)$	13.66	6.31	
	(6.52)**	(8.95)	
$ln(1 + I - DR)$			52.51
			(17.38)***
B_{-1}	−0.11	−0.17	−0.11
	(0.03)***	(0.09)**	(0.03)***
ΔR^n	−0.46	−0.06	−0.64
	(0.04)***	(0.03)*	(0.04)***
$\Delta Debits$	0.99	1.72	1.12
	(0.53)**	(0.62)**	(0.46)***
D	−10.51	−1.60	−18.60
	(5.81)**	(7.38)	(5.34)***
Adj. R^2	.57	.45	.77
Observations	109	20	89
Switchpoint[a]		0.13	0.13

notes: Standard errors are in parentheses. Adj. R^2 is the R^2 adjusted for degrees of freedom.

***, **, * indicates statistically significant at the .01, .05, and .10 levels (one-tail tests).

[a] estimate of $(I - DR)*$

Federal Reserve district (Table 3.1), and for reporting member banks in New York City (Table 3.2). On average, the New York district accounted for 25% of the borrowing of all U.S. member banks during this period. Moreover, only in this district was the discount rate below the market rate of interest (measured here as the commercial-paper rate) during the depression, and then only through May 1932.

Equation 1.1 in Table 3.1 is an ordinary least squares (OLS) estimate of the basic Goldfeld–Kane model incorporating bank debits and the depression dummy variable as additional independent variables, but ignoring the possibility of switching or nonlinearity in the

Table 3.2

The Demand for Member Bank Borrowing
New York City
January 1924-February 1933. Dependent variable: ΔB

	Eq. 2.1	Eq. 2.2	Eq. 2.3
Intercept	16.36	13.37	5.42
	(6.48)*	(4.36)***	(10.49)
$(I - DR)$	12.27	0.57	
	(7.17)**	(5.13)	
$ln(1 + I - DR)$			44.81
			(21.24)**
B_{-1}	−0.19	−0.20	−0.18
	(0.05)***	(0.07)***	(0.05)***
ΔR^n	−0.41	0.01	−0.60
	(0.05)***	(0.02)	(0.05)***
$\Delta Debits$	1.05	0.52	1.42
	(0.60)**	(0.41)	(0.58)***
D	−16.96	−12.97	−22.81
	(7.12)***	(5.87)**	(7.18)***
Adj. R^2	.45	.24	.64
Observations	109	20	89
Switchpoint⁼		0.13	0.13

notes: Standard errors are in parentheses. Adj. R^2 is the R^2 adjusted for degrees of freedom.

***, **, * indicates statistically significant at the .01, .05, and .10 levels (one-tail tests).

⁼ estimate of $(I - DR)^*$

rate spread–borrowing relationship.[14] The depression dummy is set equal to 0 from January 1924–November 1929, and equal to 1 from December 1929–February 1933.[15] All of the regression coefficients have the anticipated signs, and all are statistically significant.

---

[14] Seasonal dummy variables also were included in a second set of estimates which are not reported. They had little explanatory power, and in no way altered qualitatively the results presented in Tables 3.1 and 3.2.

[15] The initial break in the stock market came in October 1929, but was followed by other significant declines in November. Thus I chose to set the dummy variable equal to 0 in November, rather than equal to 1. The results are not affected qualitatively by setting the dummy equal to 1 beginning in October, November or December 1929, or in December 1930, at the end of the first major banking panic.

Equations 1.2 and 1.3 in Table 3.1 incorporate switching behavior and nonlinearity in the relationship between bank borrowing and the rate differential. The rate spread at which switching occurs, $(I - DR)^*$, is estimated using a search procedure to locate the spread that maximizes the value of the log-likelihood function.[16] Once determined, OLS is used to estimate the upper- and lower-regime regressions. The estimate of $(I - DR)^*$ is 0.13, and the null hypothesis of no switching can be rejected at the .01 level.[17] Further, a test of the hypothesis that the switchpoint equals zero also can be rejected (at the .02, but not .01, level).[18] This suggests that banks were reluctant to borrow from the Fed even at small positive rate differentials, as Dutkowsky's (1984) model predicts.

Equation 1.2 is an estimate of the borrowed-reserve demand function when the rate spread is less than or equal to 0.13 (i.e., an estimate of Equation 3). The coefficient estimates from this regression have the anticipated signs, and those on lagged borrowing, flows of nonborrowed reserves and bank debits are statistically significant. Equation 1.3 is an estimate of borrowed-reserve demand when the rate spread is greater than 0.13 (Equation 4). All of the coefficients have the correct signs and are statistically significant at the .01 level (except the intercept). The results suggest that for rate spreads above 0.13, bank borrowing was responsive to changes in the rate spread, to the lagged level of borrowing, and to flows of nonborrowed reserves. Moreover, they also indicate that member-bank borrowing was related positively to economic activity. As economic activity,

---

[16] Specifically, I searched for the value of $(I - DR)$ which maximizes the sum of the log-likelihood values from estimates of Equations 3 and 4. See Johnston (1984, pp. 407–09) and Dutkowsky (1984, pp. 417–18) for a further discussion of this procedure.

[17] The specific null hypothesis is a joint hypothesis of no switching and of the presence of a linear relationship between the rate spread and member-bank borrowing. That is, it is a test of the equality of all of the coefficients of Equations 1.2 with those of 1.3 (Table 2.1), with a further restriction that the coefficient on $\ln(1 + I - DR)$ in Equation 1.3 equals 0. The likelihood ratio statistic equals 73.812; the chi-square statistic with seven degrees of freedom equals 18.475 at the .01 level.

[18] The null hypothesis is that the switchpoint equals zero, against the alternative that it equals 0.13. The likelihood ratio statistic equals 5.876; the chi-square statistic with 1 degree of freedom equals 6.635 at the .01 level, and 5.412 at the .02 level.

and hence loan demand, increased, bank borrowing increased. When economic activity declined, as in the early 1930s, member-bank borrowing fell. Assuming that the coefficient of 1.12 on the change in debits is correct, the decline in debits between 1929 and 1930 can explain about 11% of the decline in the member-bank borrowing of New York district banks between these years.[19]

The coefficient on the depression dummy variable suggests that there was a significant down-shift in the borrowed-reserves demand function following the stock market crash. The shift can account for approximately 10% of the decline in borrowed reserves between 1929 and 1930, for example.[20] As the shocks to the financial system worsened, banks probably became even less willing to borrow reserves. Banks also would have been less able to borrow if they lacked sufficient eligible paper to use as collateral. Because of the change in bank willingness (or ability) to borrow from the Federal Reserve, the level of borrowed reserves became an increasingly inaccurate measure of monetary conditions. Nevertheless, Fed officials continued to interpret little borrowing as a sign of exceptional monetary ease.

Regression estimates of the demand for borrowed reserves by weekly reporting member banks in New York City from January 1924–February 1933 are reported in Table 3.2. The rate spread at which switching occurs is again estimated to be 0.13, and the null hypothesis of no switching is rejected at the .01 level.[21] Above this spread, the coefficient estimates all have the anticipated signs and are statistically significant (Equation 2.3 in Table 3.2). The results sug-

---

[19] The average monthly levels of borrowed reserves in 1929 and 1930 were $240.82 million and $58.23 million, respectively, a difference of $–182.59 million. Bank debits averaged $52.3 billion per month in 1929 and $33.8 billion in 1930, a difference of $–18.5 billion. Multiplying –18.5 by 1.12 and dividing by 182.59 gives .11, or 11%.

[20] This is calculated by dividing the coefficient –18.60 by $–182.59, the difference in the monthly average level of borrowed reserves between 1929 and 1930.

[21] The likelihood ratio test statistic equals 74.978, while the chi-square statistic with seven degrees of freedom is 18.475 at the .01 level. It was not possible to test the null hypothesis that the switchpoint equals zero because the only month prior to December 1929 when the rate spread was less than or equal to zero also happened to be the only month when New York City banks borrowed from the Fed at an unfavorable rate spread. Thus the lower-regime regression could not be estimated in the case where the switchpoint is set equal to zero.

gest further that borrowing was positively related to changes in economic activity, and that a down-shift in the demand for borrowed reserves occurred during the depression.[22] And they indicate further that the failure of Fed officials to interpret the behavior of borrowed reserves correctly contributed to their belief throughout the depression that monetary conditions were easy.

Summary

The Fed's failure to undertake significant expansionary policies during the depression resulted largely from its misreading of monetary conditions. Because Fed officials believed that the sharp decline in borrowed reserves following the stock market crash implied that money and credit were plentiful, they failed to buy a significant quantity of securities. This chapter illustrates that much of the decline in borrowed reserves was caused by the depression itself, however. Of course, a portion of the decline stemmed from an increase in nonborrowed reserves. But Fed officials failed to recognize that falling loan demand, heightened banker caution, and a lack of eligible paper, also contributed to the decrease in member-bank borrowing. Moreover, they saw no need to offset declines in borrowed reserves with further purchases of securities.

On the surface, the System's inaction during the depression appears inconsistent with its prompt and vigorous response to the recessions of 1924 and 1927. But, in fact the Fed's behavior was largely consistent throughout. The comparatively steep decline in income in 1930–31 caused a more substantial drop in member-bank borrowing in those years than had occurred in 1924 and 1927. Consequently, although they bought fewer securities, Fed officials believed that they were being as responsive to the depression as they had been in 1924 and 1927. The Fed's strategy was procyclical. Indeed, because of the procyclical nature of member-bank borrow-

---

[22] The decline in debits between 1929 and 1930 can account for approximately 18% of the decline in borrowed reserves between those two years. And the down-shift in the borrowed reserve demand function can explain about 16% of the decline (see footnote 19 for the calculation method).

ing, the Fed tended to purchase *fewer* securities the *worse* an economic downturn was. During mild recessions, as in 1927, member-bank borrowing fell little. The Fed responded with relatively heavy purchases of securities, however, interpreting monetary conditions as tight. But during severe downturns, as in 1930–31, member-bank borrowing declined substantially. This caused the Fed to interpret monetary conditions as relatively easy, however, and hence to make comparatively few open-market purchases.

4. Policy disagreements within the Federal Reserve System: the effects of institutional change

> [G]o back to 1927 when the last great open-market blunder was made by the Federal Reserve System. . . . It was an operation that was initiated, proposed, and developed by the Federal Reserve Bank of New York. . . . I doubt whether, if the Federal Reserve Board at that time had been clothed with the exclusive power [over open-market policy], . . . the Board would have dared to venture upon that operation.
>
> Adolph Miller (United States Senate 1935, p. 689)

The preceding chapter concludes that Federal Reserve policy during the Great Depression was largely predictable from the Fed's statements and actions during the 1920s. Thus, it suggests that the organizational changes stressed by Friedman and Schwartz (1963) – Benjamin Strong's death and reorganization of the Open Market Committee – played only a minor role in the System's mistakes during the depression. Nevertheless, it is true that during the depression officials of the Federal Reserve Bank of New York often proposed more expansionary actions than were accepted by the rest of the System. While it is certainly not clear that the Fed would have acted with sufficient vigor to halt the depression and promote recovery, monetary policy would undoubtedly have been more responsive had New York retained its leadership position.

This chapter studies the disagreements within the Federal Reserve System in order to better understand the impact of organizational changes on policy during the depression. First, I explore the impact of the ambiguous relationship between the Federal Reserve Board and the Reserve Banks. During the 1920s the Federal Reserve Bank of New York dominated policy making, with the Board and other Reserve Banks generally acquiescing. But, during the depression the

Reserve Banks did not follow the New York Fed in lowering their discount and acceptance buying rates, and the Open Market Committee failed to approve many of the open-market purchases proposed by New York. This chapter seeks to explain both the lack of uniformity in the discount rates of the Reserve Banks, as well as the reluctance of many officials to use open-market operations during the depression.

The struggle for power

The twelve Federal Reserve Banks are one vestige of the original design of the Federal Reserve System. The system of regional Banks, with a central supervising board, was a compromise between proponents of a central bank, modeled after European central banks, and those favoring a loose confederation of regional banks, which were responsive solely to the credit needs of their local districts (Timberlake 1978, pp. 186–99). A majority of the directors of each Bank was appointed from within the local district, and each Reserve Bank set its own discount and acceptance-buying rates, subject to Federal Reserve Board approval, and was free to engage in open-market operations as it wished.

The relationship between the Federal Reserve Banks and the Federal Reserve Board was unclear, and this ambiguity made it difficult to formulate policy and to respond quickly and forcefully to crises: "Experience . . . demonstrated the dangers of a system in which power and responsibility were diffused in an ambiguous way among the Board and the 12 Reserve banks, with no one body clearly empowered to take the initiative for the system as a whole or to force unified action" (Chandler 1971, p. 89).

The Board's role was largely supervisory. It could approve or disapprove discount and acceptance-rate changes and open-market operations proposed by the Reserve Banks, but whether it had the authority to initiate policy was less clear. Before the Senate Banking Committee in 1935, Charles Hamlin, a member of the Federal Reserve Board from the System's inception, testified:

The Federal Reserve Act established 12 regional banks with the Federal Reserve Board as the supervisory, controlling authority. As a matter of fact, each one of those Federal Reserve banks essentially is a central bank with autonomy of its own. It has practically all the powers that any central bank in Europe has. (United States Senate 1935, p. 942)

But, based on advice from the Board's counsel, Hamlin claimed also that the Board did have the power to initiate open-market operations, although "as a matter of fact, we never exercised or tried to exercise that power. . . . [It] depended on a somewhat involved construction of the act" (ibid., p. 945). However, Adolph Miller, another charter member of the Board, testified that "the Board never has had the full responsibility . . . to initiate an open-market operation" (ibid., p. 690).

In January and February 1931 a subcommittee of the Senate Committee on Banking and Currency conducted hearings on the *Operation of the National and Federal Reserve Banking Systems*. The hearings were chaired by Carter Glass, one of the principal authors of the Federal Reserve Act, and a member of the Federal Reserve Board as Treasury Secretary during the Wilson Administration. Glass strongly supported the autonomy of the individual Reserve Banks. Adolph Miller was critical of the open-market purchases of 1924 and 1927, and played to Glass' convictions when he suggested that the operations had violated the intent of Congress:

Miller: "I want to call the attention of the committee to this, that whenever the Federal reserve system operates through the open-market committee, it operates, in effect, as a central bank."

Glass: "Which it was never intended to be."

Miller: "You strip your regional banks of their separate control of credit in their several districts when you operate with their resources in the central money market of the country" (United States Senate 1931, p. 140).

Miller argued that the Federal Reserve Board should be given full authority over open-market operations in order to prevent future inappropriate operations:

I have no hesitation in telling the committee that, in my judgement, the safety of the Federal reserve system for the country depends very largely upon . . . the men who constitute the Federal Reserve Board. . . . [A] group of conscientious men, of high character and good intelligence, sitting constantly with these problems, somewhat remote from the atmosphere of the great centers, is capable of an objective and detached view, such as the ablest of men are seldom capable of when they are right in the atmosphere of the large centers and engrossed in their own affairs. (ibid., p. 133)

Glass remained opposed to centralized control of monetary policy, whether in the hands of the Open Market Committee or the Federal Reserve Board, as he reiterated during hearings on the Banking Act of 1935: "I think that we have determined . . . that this country does not want a central bank" (United States Senate 1935, p.83). He argued against a proposal to permit the Federal Reserve Board to compel the participation of individual Reserve Banks in System open-market operations, contending that the Reserve Banks understood best whether open-market operations would be beneficial to their local districts (ibid., pp. 81, 945). However, Glass did stress that the Federal Reserve Act had given the Board considerable power over the Reserve Banks, including the ability to veto proposed open-market operations. And he complained that the Board had not exercised that power often enough: "they have as a Board exhibited a lamentable degree of timidity at times where courage was required" (ibid., p. 876).[1] Referring to the open-market purchases of 1927 he stated, "that was, in my judgement, a distinct departure from both the text and the spirit of the Federal Reserve Act, without one particle of lawful sanction. . . . [And] the Board had full responsibility [for approving or disapproving the operation]" (ibid., pp. 689–90).

Whether or not the Federal Reserve Board had the authority to force the Reserve Banks to change their discount rates also was unclear. In October 1927 the Board had ordered the Federal Reserve Bank of Chicago to reduce its discount rate, and the Bank complied. Glass was adamant that the Board did not have this authority: "It was

---

[1] Also see his exchange with Miller in United States Senate (1931, pp. 133–34).

never the intent that the board should initiate the discount rate" (United States Senate 1931, p. 179).[2] But he was equally certain that the Board had the power, indeed the responsibility, to determine the type of paper eligible for rediscount and to force the Reserve Banks to refuse discount loans to member banks which the Board believed had abused the borrowing privilege (ibid., pp. 140–44).[3]

Because the Federal Reserve Act failed to make clear the distribution of authority within the System, and perhaps because of some hesitation on the part of its members, the Federal Reserve Board did not exercise much influence on policy in the System's early years. During the war the Treasury dominated, with the Secretary of the Treasury serving as *ex officio* chairman of the Federal Reserve Board.[4] Later, because of his stature and personality, Benjamin Strong emerged as the System's leader. The New York Fed's power was enhanced by the relative size of its member banks and their position in the international financial market. And the "discovery" of open-market operations in the early 1920s further solidified New York's position, as the operations of the Reserve Banks were brought under the authority of a Governors Committee, and later the Open Market Investment Committee, both of which Strong headed. While there were occasional disagreements among the Reserve Banks, and between the Banks and Federal Reserve Board, the Federal Reserve Bank of New York largely dictated policy throughout much of the 1920s.[5]

The New York Fed's influence began to decline in 1928 over

---

[2] Glass held a decidedly different opinion in November and December 1919 when he was a member of the Federal Reserve Board as Treasury Secretary. On that occasion he opposed rate increases proposed by Benjamin Strong, declared that the Board had the power to impose a discount rate on a Reserve Bank and sought an opinion from the Attorney General to support him (Chandler 1958, pp. 148–65).

[3] One provision of the Banking Act of 1933 made clear the Board's right to limit discount-window access to member banks carrying stock market loans.

[4] The Banking Act of 1935 removed the Secretary of the Treasury from the Board effective February 1, 1936.

[5] See Chandler (1958, pp. 41–187) and Wicker (1966a, pp. 3–45) for descriptions of the power struggles within the Federal Reserve, and between the Fed and the Treasury, during the System's early years.

disagreement about how, or even whether, to respond to stock market speculation. Strong apparently argued against any attempt to influence stock market activity, but illness and a focus on international monetary reconstruction limited his influence on domestic policy issues. To the extent that a response was necessary, Strong favored discount rate increases to discourage the financing of speculation with Federal Reserve credit. Several of the Reserve Banks increased their discount rates to 5% in 1928. But, not wanting to increase the cost of credit for "legitimate" borrowers, the Federal Reserve Board disapproved the applications of the New York and other Reserve Banks to increase their rates to 6% in early 1929. Instead, the Board directed the Reserve Banks to pursue a policy of "direct pressure," in which discount loans simply were refused to any bank carrying stock market loans. The Reserve Banks, especially the Federal Reserve Bank of New York, countered that it was impossible to control the use of reserves supplied by discount loans. The disagreement meant that neither response was implemented fully, and, as a consequence, System policy was "clearly too easy to stem the bull market and almost surely too tight to permit the continued expansion of business activity without severe downward pressure on prices" (Friedman and Schwartz 1963, pp. 265–66).[6]

The Federal Reserve was similarly paralyzed during the Great Depression. Some members of the Federal Reserve Board supported the proposals for expansionary operations advocated by the New York Fed, but were unable to convince a majority of either the Board or Open Market Committee. Its success in forcing the Federal Reserve Bank of Chicago to lower its discount rate in 1927 had enhanced the Board's control of policy. Yet, its inability to fully implement the "direct pressure" policy to fight stock market speculation, or to sway a majority of the Reserve Banks to support expansionary policies during the depression demonstrates just how little power the Board possessed.

The Banking Act of 1935 ultimately settled the question of power in favor of the Federal Reserve Board. While there remained con-

---

[6] Field (1984a, 1984b) and Hamilton (1987) contend that the Fed's policies in 1928 and 1929 were particularly important causes of the subsequent depression.

siderable resistance to consolidation of power within the Board, particularly from Carter Glass, it was generally agreed that the failures of Federal Reserve policy during the depression had stemmed in part from the diffuse distribution of authority within the System. While Marriner Eccles, whom Franklin Roosevelt had appointed Governor of the Federal Reserve Board in 1933, argued that in some respects the Banking Act enhanced the autonomy of the Reserve Banks, in fact the Banks lost virtually all say in monetary policy making.[7] The Board was given control of the Open Market Committee, and its authority to compel the Reserve Banks to change their discount rates was made clear.[8]

Discount policy of the Reserve Banks

One feature of Federal Reserve policy before 1935 was a lack of uniformity among the discount rates of the different Federal Reserve Banks. Indeed, when surveyed by the Senate Banking Committee in 1931, all of the Reserve Banks, save New York, opposed unambiguously a uniform national discount rate. The Federal Reserve Bank of San Francisco explained:

If there were one rate uniform in all districts, it would usually be a rate determined in the principal money center, New York, and usually be an improper rate in many other districts. There should also be at times variation influencing the flow of funds from one district or section to another. (United States Senate 1931, p. 778)

And the Dallas Reserve Bank responded: "If rates were arbitrarily made uniform it would destroy the principle of having 12 reserve banks and tend to establish a central bank principle" (ibid., p. 777).

While opposing uniform rates in principle, the Reserve Banks did consider national monetary policy goals when fixing their discount

[7] See Eccles' testimony in United States Senate (1935, pp. 279–325).

[8] See Chandler (1971, pp. 305–07) for a summary of the changes brought about by this act.

rates, and rate changes often were coordinated among the Banks.[9] Nevertheless, at times there were substantial disagreements among them. Given the degree of autonomy each Bank had in setting its discount rate, differences in their rates likely reflected in part these disagreements.

Figure 4.1 plots the discount rate of the Federal Reserve Bank of New York against the average rate of all eleven other Reserve Banks. Typically, the New York rate was below those of the other Banks. As demonstrated in Chapter 2, the Federal Reserve Bank of New York adjusted its discount rate when it was deemed too far out of line with market rates. Thus, to some extent New York's relatively low discount rate probably reflected the fact that market interest rates were usually lower in New York than elsewhere.[10]

Figures 4.2 and 4.3 compare the discount rates of the Chicago and San Francisco Reserve Banks with that of New York. Officials of both Banks often disagreed strongly with the policies advocated by New York, and these disagreements likely contributed to differences between the discount rates of these Banks and that of New York. Chicago was one of seven Reserve Banks that did not reduce its discount rate below 4% during the 1924 recession. Only New York reduced its rate to 3%, while Boston, Philadelphia, Cleveland, and San Francisco all reduced to 3.5%. In response to a 1931 Senate Banking Committee inquiry into monetary policy, most of the Reserve Banks explained that their discount rate reductions in 1924 were intended to stimulate borrowing and economic activity. For example, the St. Louis Bank responded, "we hoped to give agriculture and business the benefit of a lower rate in crop-moving time" (ibid., p. 764). Chicago's explanation suggests its officers were skep-

---

[9] Econometric analysis of discount rate changes of each Reserve Bank suggests that the variables that explain changes in the discount rate of the Federal Reserve Bank of New York – the difference between the discount rate and market rates, changes in industrial production, and international gold flows – also influenced discount-rate policy in the other Reserve Banks. However, this analysis does not indicate whether the Banks had the same policy objectives, or whether they simply were following New York's lead in order to limit undesired reserve flows between districts.

[10] This is not to say that the generally lower discount rate in New York did not contribute to lower market rates in that district.

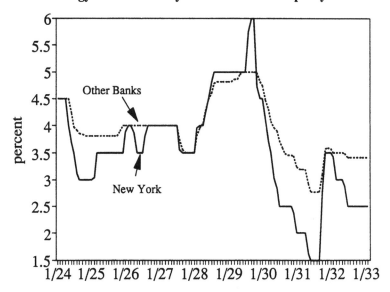

January 1924--February 1933

Figure 4.1. Discount rate: Federal Reserve Bank of New York and average rate of all other Federal Reserve Banks.

tical about reducing their discount rate, but did so "inasmuch as there was very little speculative demand for credit that no harm could be done by reducing the rate to 4% and that it might help business, which was reported as being rather dull at that time" (ibid., p. 756).

Discount rates were relatively uniform throughout the rest of the 1920s. That did not reflect general agreement about policy, however. The reduction to 3.5% by all Banks in 1927 was part of a System-wide policy to repel gold flows from England and to stimulate domestic economic activity.[11] But Chicago reduced its rate only after having been ordered to do so by the Federal Reserve Board, and it was first to return its rate to 4%. Responding to the Senate Banking Committee survey, the Chicago Bank explained: "At that time [1927] our board felt that a reduction in the rate would cause further ex-

[11] The responses to the Senate Banking Committee survey in 1931 make this clear. See United States Senate (1931, pp. 752–64).

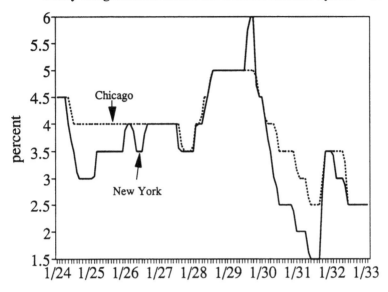

January 1924--February 1933

Figure 4.2. Discount rate: Federal Reserve Bank of New York and Federal Reserve Bank of Chicago.

pansion of speculative credit. Whatever good purposes might be served would be more than offset by the disastrous consequences of a further inflation of security prices" (ibid., p. 756). San Francisco had also reduced its rate under pressure from the Federal Reserve Board. It increased the rate in February 1928 when, "in light of subsequent events, [the earlier reduction] was found to have been a mistake" (ibid., p. 764).

All of the Reserve Banks initiated discount-rate increases in early 1928, primarily because of heightened concern about stock market speculation. The Atlanta Fed explained that its increases were "to restrain the prevalent speculative tendency" (ibid., p. 753). And St. Louis replied that it was necessary to increase its discount rate because "we were in danger of burdening this district with borrowing that belonged to other districts" (ibid., p. 764).

In an attempt to slow the flow of funds to Wall Street, the discount

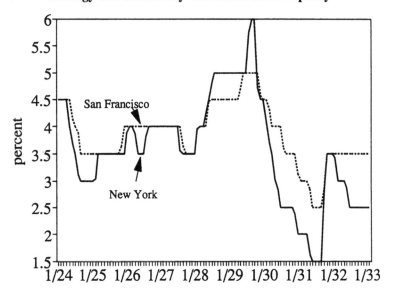

January 1924--February 1933

Figure 4.3. Discount rate: Federal Reserve Bank of New York and Federal Reserve Bank of San Francisco.

rate of the Federal Reserve Bank of New York was kept at 4% for four weeks after Chicago and Boston had raised their rates to 4.5% on April 20, 1928.[12] And, while this attempt to control the flow of funds was apparently deemed a failure, the Reserve Banks continued to believe that differences in their rates influenced the flow of funds between districts. While most of the Banks had increased their discount rates to 5% by mid-1928, the Minneapolis, Kansas City, Dal-

---

[12] Four other Reserve Banks increased their discount rates between April 20 and May 18, when the New York increase took effect. A cable from Federal Reserve Bank of Dallas Chairman Walsh to the Federal Reserve Board on May 7, 1928 in support of the Bank's application for a discount-rate increase explains their objective: "It was estimated that not less than one hundred millions of dollars is now being loaned on the call market in New York from the eleventh district. . . . [It] would tend to curb speculation on New York market if the other 11 districts should increase their rates above New York and thus be the means of requiring many call loans in this district to be retired and returned for legitimate demands here" (United States Senate 1931, p. 758). Also see Chandler (1971, p. 45).

las, and San Francisco Banks kept their rates at 4.5% until May 1929. Kansas City later explained why it had increased its rate to 5% in that month:

It was felt that our maintenance of a rate lower than that of nine of the other Federal reserve banks was not benefitting the industry of the district, since the generally higher rates prevailing throughout the country were preventing our lower rate from being passed on, in any noticeable degree, to the borrowers from our member banks. The abnormally high rates prevailing in eastern centers were forcing an unusual demand for loans on the larger banks of our district, from large concerns having contacts and credit lines with our banks, but which under normal conditions do their borrowing in the open market or from eastern banks. (ibid., p. 760)

The Federal Reserve Board refused to permit discount rates to be set above 5% until August, when New York was authorized to raise its rate to 6%. This action was decided upon following a meeting of the governors of all twelve Reserve Banks and the Federal Reserve Board on August 7 and 8. All of the governors, except New York Fed Governor George Harrison, opposed discount rate increases at their own Banks, although a majority favored an increase in the New York rate (Chandler 1971, p. 73). Apparently some of the governors feared that an increase in the New York rate would generate an increased flow of funds away from their districts. Throughout 1928 and 1929 the Reserve Banks were concerned about declines in their reserve ratios caused by such flows, and were apprehensive that the New York rate increase would force them into rate increases of their own.

Following the stock market crash the Federal Reserve Bank of New York reduced its discount rate to 5% on November 1, and then to 4.5% on November 15. Boston and Chicago reduced their rates to 4.5% a week later, and three more Reserve Banks followed by year's end. New York continued to cut its rate aggressively, although during the first half of 1930 the Federal Reserve Board disapproved some of the reductions proposed by New York.

The other Reserve Banks were more cautious about reducing their discount rates, and many cut their rates only because of New York's prior reductions. For example, of the three rate reductions made by the Chicago Fed between November 1929 and January 1931, Governor McDougal explained that the first two were taken to improve business conditions, while the final had been only to narrow the differential with New York, which he believed had reduced its rate too much (ibid., p. 135).[13] By May 1931, when the final round of rate reductions was made, the discount rate of the Federal Reserve Bank of New York stood at 1.5%. The Boston rate was 2%, the Cleveland, Chicago, St. Louis, and San Francisco rates were 2.5%, the Philadelphia, Richmond, Atlanta, Kansas City, and Dallas rates were 3%, and the Minneapolis rate was 3.5%. It is unclear why the Reserve Banks resisted discount rate reductions; money market rates had fallen sharply and member-bank borrowing was low. Moreover, Fed officials seem to have preferred that Federal Reserve credit expand through discount loans (or bill purchases), rather than through purchases of government securities. Yet, outside New York, none of the Reserve Banks had lowered its discount rate sufficiently to stimulate borrowing or economic recovery. Why did the Reserve Banks maintain contractionary discount rate policies in the face of unprecedented economic depression?

The determinants of Reserve Bank discount rates

The Senate Banking Committee's 1931 survey of Federal Reserve Bank policies provides some insight into the reasons for discount-rate changes. The Federal Reserve Bank of Boston's reply indicates that among the factors influencing its discount-rate setting were the Bank's reserve ratio relative to the ratio of the System as a whole, the relation of the discount rate to market interest rates, the flow of funds between districts, and business conditions, both locally and throughout the country. For example, the Bank's discount rate cut in June 1924 was explained as follows:

At the time this rate was reduced the country at large was in a state of depression. . . . In New England this was felt in the shoe and leather and the cotton industries. . . . Open-market money rates . . . were out of line with the

---

[13] Also see Chicago's explanation to the Senate Banking Committee in United States Senate (1931, p. 756).

discount rate, being substantially below it. . . . On June 11 the reserve ratio
of the Federal Reserve Bank of Boston was 87.5 per cent and of the system
82.4 per cent. (United States Senate 1931, p. 753)

And, explaining its discount rate increase in September, 1925, the
Bank replied: "From the summer of 1924 to this date there had been
a steady increase in business activity here in New England. . . .
[O]pen money market rates had gotten out of line with the discount
rate" (ibid., p. 753). A further rate increase in November 1925 was
justified by the Bank's low reserve ratio relative to that of the System
as a whole (ibid., p. 754). The Bank's other rate changes were
justified similarly.

Many of the Reserve Banks explained their discount-rate adjustments as responses to changes in market interest rates and to discount-rate changes by other Reserve Banks. For example, the Federal
Reserve Bank of Dallas justified its rate reduction in August, 1924 as
follows:

The stronger and larger banks which normally come into the market for
some credit at that season appeared to be making their arrangements according to the best advantage with reference to rates. Our committee felt that the
facilities of this bank should not be made unavailable to member banks by
reason of the opportunity to fill their needs elsewhere at a lower cost. (ibid.,
pp. 757–58)

The Kansas City Fed listed its strong reserve position, lower market
rates, and a desire to "encourage" business as justifications for rate
reductions in 1930 (ibid., p. 760). The Philadelphia Bank also explained many of its rate adjustments as caused by changes in market
rates, while its discount rate increase in 1928 resulted from "adverse
trade balances of this district, as a result of which the bank was losing
gold" (ibid: 763).

Several of the Reserve Banks wrote that rate changes were forced
on them by the actions of other Banks. For example, the St. Louis Fed
explained that "on February 11, 1930, we were the last of the reserve
banks to decrease our rate to 4.5 per cent and were forced to do so
largely by the action of our neighboring districts" (ibid., p. 764). And
the San Francisco Fed summarized the reasons for its rate reduction
on August 8, 1930 as follows: "Economic situation appears to be

increasingly serious; San Francisco rate out of line with Federal reserve banks which may properly be classed with San Francisco; wide spread between discount rate and bill rates obviously inconsistent; reserves (87 per cent) also above average of system [sic]" (ibid., p. 764).

In sum, the factors listed most frequently by the Reserve Banks to explain their discount rate adjustments included 1) a desire (or necessity) to conform with changes made by other Reserve Banks; 2) changes in market interest rates; 3) unusual (or undesirable) amounts of borrowing by member banks and their customers in the district, and hence an unusual (or undesirable) flow of funds between districts; and 4) a desire to affect local economic conditions. Can these factors account for the differences between the discount rates of the Reserve Banks during the depression?

A model of Reserve Bank discount-rate policy

To explore further the lack of uniformity in the discount rates of the Federal Reserve Banks, I estimate an econometric model of the difference between the discount rate of each Reserve Bank (indexed by i) and that of the Federal Reserve Bank of New York ($DR_i - DR_{NY}$).

The Reserve Bank replies to the Senate Banking Committee survey indicate that discount-rate adjustments followed changes in market interest rates. And, as suggested above, regional differences in market interest rates could account for the lack of uniformity in discount rates. To test this possibility, I include the difference between the commercial-loan rate in each district and the commercial-loan rate in New York, lagged one period, $(ICL_i - ICL_{NY})_{-1}$ as an independent variable. It is expected that an increase in this differential, for example, would lead to an increase in the difference between the discount rate of Bank i and the New York discount rate. Hence, its coefficient should be positive.

Reserve Bank officials believed that differences in their discount rates influenced the flow of funds between districts. Their attempt to limit the flow of funds to Wall Street in 1928 by increasing interest rates outside New York was but one instance when the Fed used discount rates to affect reserve flows. During the depression the Reserve Banks again were concerned with the flow of reserves to New York, and it seems likely that the outlying Reserve districts were slow to cut their discount rates in order to limit these flows. Figure 4.4 illustrates that New York's shares of member bank total and nonborrowed reserves increased from late 1927 to the end of 1932, the only exception being in the wake of the stock market crash. In not reducing their discount rates along with the New York Fed in the 1930s, the Reserve Banks might have been attempting to limit this redistribution of reserves. Unfortunately, the upward bias on discount rates created by these attempts exacerbated the decline in the supply of money, and hence worsened the depression.

Eichengreen (1984) presents a game-theoretic model of central-bank interaction under the interwar gold standard that suggests fur-

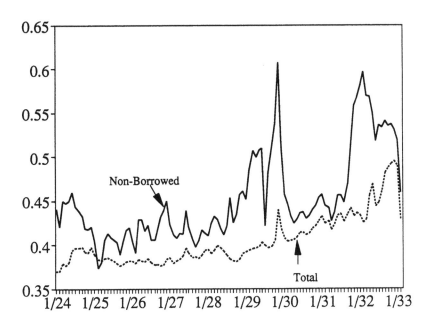

January 1924--February 1933

Figure 4.4. New York District shares of member-bank reserves.

ther that competition for reserves might explain discount-rate differences during the depression. In the model each central bank is assumed to be concerned with its gold reserves and with domestic economic stability, but has only one policy instrument, its discount rate. In the absence of cooperation, central banks compete for gold, discount rates are set higher than they would be otherwise, and a deflationary bias results. But if central banks cooperate, or if one bank assumes a leadership role, discount rates are set lower and there is less deflation. Eichengreen documents the inability of England and France to cooperate on a solution to England's chronic payments deficits in 1927 and 1928, and implies that the severity of the Great Depression stemmed in part from a general lack of central-bank cooperation.

As between European central banks, there was a decided lack of cooperation among the Federal Reserve Banks during the depression. Friedman and Schwartz (1963, p. 415) argue that officials outside of New York "tended to be jealous of New York and predisposed to question what New York proposed." And they held "resentment at New York's failure to carry the day in 1929 and [had] the feeling that existing difficulties were the proper punishment for the System's past misdeeds in not checking the bull market" (ibid., p. 372). Further suggesting an absence of cooperation, Epstein and Ferguson (1984, pp. 972–73) document occasional unwillingness of some Reserve Banks to lend *their* gold to those which were running low.[14] The lack of cooperation among the Reserve Banks probably kept discount rates higher than they would have been otherwise, and hence exacerbated the monetary collapse.

To capture the possible effect on discount rates of changes in the distribution of reserves among Fed districts, I include the ratio of total member-bank reserves in each district to total reserves of all U.S. member banks, lagged one period ($Rshare_{i-1}$), as an independent variable.[15] If a Reserve Bank increased its discount rate (relative to

---

[14] Emphasis in original. See Chandler (1971, pp. 186–90) for further evidence.

[15] Although much of the flow of reserves was toward the New York district, the Reserve Banks would likely have been concerned with their reserve shares relative to all other districts, not just New York. Hence the choice of this variable.

the New York discount rate) in response to a decline in its district's reserve share, the sign of this variable's coefficient should be negative.

As an alternative to the district's member-bank reserve share, I also include as an explanatory variable the difference between the Reserve Bank's own reserve ratio and the reserve ratio of the Federal Reserve System as a whole, lagged one period ($Rratio_i - Rratio_{US})_{-1}$. Several of the Reserve Banks indicated that this difference influenced their rate policy, and a lack of reserves appears to have prevented some of them from participating fully in expansionary policies in late 1931 and in 1932 (Chandler 1971, pp. 186–91, 199; Epstein and Ferguson 1984, pp. 972–73). Accordingly, I expect a negative coefficient on this variable, reflecting a discount rate increase (relative to New York) if a district's reserve ratio declined relative to that of the System as a whole.[16]

It seems reasonable to expect that the Reserve Banks also responded to local economic conditions. Hence, discount rates might have been set lower in districts suffering relatively more economic distress. To test this hypothesis, I include the difference between the percentage change in bank debits in each district and the percentage change for the U.S. as a whole, lagged one period, ($Debits_i - Debits_{US})_{-1}$ as an additional independent variable.[17] If, for example, a Reserve Bank reduced its discount rate relative to the New York discount rate in response to slower than average economic growth, then the coefficient of this variable should be positive.[18] Finally, I include the lagged discount rate differential ($DR_i - DR_{NY})_{-1}$ as an explanatory variable. Throughout its history, the Federal Reserve Banks have changed their discount rates relatively infrequently, and

---

[16] I experimented with using the difference between a district's reserve ratio and that of the Federal Reserve Bank of New York. The estimates were not substantially different and are not reported here.

[17] Specifically, the percentage change in bank debits is measured as the difference between the log of debits in the current month and the log of debits twelve months previous. The debits data for the U.S. as a whole are debits in 141 cities minus debits in New York City. This is a commonly used measure of economic activity. See Schwartz (1981), for example.

[18] Implicitly I assume that the Federal Reserve Bank of New York responded to changes in economic activity for the nation as a whole.

during the 1920s and early 1930s there was considerable persistence of the rate differentials.[19]

The complete model of the difference between the discount rate of Reserve Bank i and the discount rate of the Federal Reserve Bank of New York is:

$$(DR_i - DR_{NY}) = \alpha_0 + \alpha_1(DR_i - DR_{NY})_{-1} + \alpha_2(ICL_i - ICL_{NY})_{-1}$$
$$+ \alpha_3(Rshare_i)_{-1} + \alpha_4(Rratio_i - Rratio_{US})_{-1}$$
$$+ \alpha_5(Debits_i - Debits_{US})_{-1} + e. \qquad (1)$$

The coefficient signs are expected to be: α_1, α_2, $\alpha_5 > 0$, and $\alpha_3 < 0$, $\alpha_4 < 0$. Monthly data are used to estimate the model.[20]

Regression estimates for January 1924–September 1931 are reported in Table 4.1, and estimates for January 1924–February 1933 are reported in Table 4.2.[21] The former period excludes the crisis triggered by Great Britain's abandonment of the gold standard and the abrupt discount-rate increases by most of the Reserve Banks. It also excludes 1932, when a lack of gold reserves seems to have constrained the operations of some of the Reserve Banks, and hence may have caused their discount-rate policies to be different from those of prior years.

For January 1924–September 1931, the regressions generally are consistent with expectations. The coefficient on the lagged dependent variable is positive and statistically significant in twenty of the regressions (of twenty-two possible), illustrating the persistence of discount-rate differentials over time. The coefficient on the commercial-loan interest rate differential is positive in all of the regressions,

---

[19] The extent to which the rate differentials were constant should not be overstated, however, since a change in the discount rate of either district i or New York produced a change in the rate differential (unless the rates were changed by the same amount on the same day, an event which occurred rarely).

[20] The discount rate observations of each Bank are averages of the rates in effect during a month, weighted by the number of days each rate was in effect.

[21] Each regression was estimated using ordinary least squares (OLS). In cases where the Durbin's-h (D-h) test indicated the presence of serially correlated errors the models were reestimated using an instrumental variables (IV) procedure.

Table 4.1

Reserve Bank Discount Rate Policies
January 1924-September 1931. Dependent variable: $DR_i - DR_{NY}$

District:	Boston	Boston	Phila.	Phila.
Intercept	−0.08 (1.37)	0.03 (0.02)	0.72 (0.89)	0.02 (0.03)
$(DR_i - DR_{NY})_{-1}$	−0.14 (0.28)	0.80 (0.07)•••	0.91 (0.05)•••	0.90 (0.06)•••
$(ICL_i - ICL_{NY})_{-1}$	0.07 (0.10)	0.11 (0.10)	0.18 (0.12)•	0.19 (0.13)•
$(Rshare_i)_{-1}$	4.12 (21.39)		−11.85 (15.07)	
$(Rratio_i - Rratio_{US})_{-1}$		0.003 (0.004)		0.001 (0.006)
$(Debits_i - Debits_{US})_{-1}$	−0.61 (0.42)	0.02 (0.33)	−0.06 (0.50)	−0.09 (0.51)
ρ	−0.74 (0.07)•••			
D-h		1.242	0.516	0.784
R^2	.64	.64	.84	.83
Observations	93	93	93	93
Method	IV	OLS	OLS	OLS

District:	Cleveland	Cleveland	Richmond	Richmond
Intercept	2.29 (0.94)••	0.02 (0.04)	2.56 (1.09)••	0.20 (0.14)
$(DR_i - DR_{NY})_{-1}$	0.93 (0.04)•••	0.93 (0.04)•••	0.57 (0.13)•••	0.44 (0.13)•••
$(ICL_i - ICL_{NY})_{-1}$	0.06 (0.06)	0.06 (0.05)	0.14 (0.07)••	0.09 (0.08)
$(Rshare_i)_{-1}$	−28.48 (11.89)•••		−84.43 (36.43)••	
$(Rratio_i - Rratio_{US})_{-1}$		−0.025 (0.007)•••		0.001 (0.006)
$(Debits_i - Debits_{US})_{-1}$	0.70 (0.44)•	0.66 (0.42)•	−0.01 (0.50)	0.62 (0.54)
ρ			−0.73 (0.07)•••	−0.74 (0.07)•••
D-h	1.015	1.252		
R^2	.87	.88	.88	.85
Observations	93	93	93	93
Method	OLS	OLS	IV	IV

(*continued*)

Strategy and consistency of Federal Reserve policy

Table 4.1, cont.

Reserve Bank Discount Rate Policies
January 1924-September 1931. Dependent Variable: $DR_i - DR_{NY}$

District:	Atlanta	Atlanta	Chicago	Chicago
Intercept	0.62	−0.02	1.04	0.03
	(0.25)**	(0.08)	(1.10)	(0.04)
$(DR_i - DR_{NY})_{-1}$	0.83	0.94	0.83	0.85
	(0.07)***	(0.05)***	(0.06)***	(0.05)***
$(ICL_i - ICL_{NY})_{-1}$	0.17	0.08	0.20	0.20
	(0.09)**	(0.10)	(0.13)*	(0.13)*
$(Rshare_i)_{-1}$	−23.10		−6.94	
	(8.75)***		(7.48)	
$(Rratio_i - Rratio_{US})_{-1}$		−0.001		−0.001
		(0.004)		(0.007)
$(Debits_i - Debits_{US})_{-1}$	0.56	0.17	−0.47	−0.64
	(0.38)*	(0.37)	(0.65)	(0.64)
ρ				
D-h	0.105	1.028	1.183	1.225
R^2	.89	.88	.83	.83
Observations	93	93	93	93
Method	OLS	OLS	OLS	OLS
District:	St. Louis	St. Louis	Minn.	Minn.
Intercept	1.96	0.12	3.11	0.25
	(0.98)**	(0.05)**	(0.99)***	(0.15)*
$(DR_i - DR_{NY})_{-1}$	0.43	0.83	−0.10	0.34
	(0.12)***	(0.05)***	(0.14)	(0.10)***
$(ICL_i - ICL_{NY})_{-1}$	0.29	0.22	0.07	0.00
	(0.12)***	(0.11)**	(0.11)	(0.11)
$(Rshare_i)_{-1}$	−52.51		−112.99	
	(27.83)**		(42.44)***	
$(Rratio_i - Rratio_{US})_{-1}$		0.008		−0.016
		(0.003)		(0.007)***
$(Debits_i - Debits_{US})_{-1}$	0.21	0.42	−0.16	0.25
	(0.54)	(0.56)	(0.35)	(0.36)
ρ	−0.74		−0.90	−0.82
	(0.07)***		(0.05)***	(0.06)***
D-h		1.585		
R^2	.84	.84	.89	.89
Observations	93	93	93	93
Method	IV	OLS	IV	IV

(continued)

Table 4.1, cont.

Reserve Bank Discount Rate Policies
January 1924-September 1931. Dependent variable: $DR_i - DR_{NY}$

District:	K. City	K. City	Dallas	Dallas
Intercept	2.26	−0.12	1.86	−0.04
	(0.55)•••	(0.13)	(0.95)•	(0.14)
$(DR_i - DR_{NY})_{-1}$	0.67	0.44	0.32	0.43
	(0.07)•••	(0.10)•••	(0.13)•••	(0.11)•••
$(ICL_i - ICL_{NY})_{-1}$	0.29	0.22	0.07	0.00
	(0.12)•••	(0.11)••	(0.11)	(0.11)
$(Rshare_i)_{-1}$	−61.18		−64.79	
	(14.36)•••		(33.67)••	
$(Rratio_i - Rratio_{US})_{-1}$		−0.017		−0.002
		(0.006)•••		(0.006)
$(ICL_i - ICL_{NY})_{-1}$	0.29	0.22	0.07	0.00
	(0.12)•••	(0.11)••	(0.11)	(0.11)
$(ICL_i - ICL_{NY})_{-1}$	0.37	0.28	0.21	0.32
	(0.09)•••	(0.11)•••	(0.09)••	(0.10)•••
$(Debits_i - Debits_{US})_{-1}$	0.78	0.24	−0.14	−0.25
	(0.43)••	(0.57)	(0.63)	(0.70)
ρ		−0.77	−0.70	−0.63
		(0.07)•••	(0.08)•••	(0.08)•••
D-h	1.017			
R^2	.90	.89	.86	.83
Observations	93	93	93	93
Method	OLS	IV	IV	IV

Table 4.1, cont.

Reserve Bank Discount Rate Policies
January 1924-September 1931. Dependent variable: $DR_i - DR_{NY}$

District:	San Francisco	San Francisco
Intercept	0.48 (1.20)	−0.01 (0.05)
$(DR_i - DR_{NY})_{-1}$	0.83 (0.07)***	0.85 (0.07)***
$(ICL_i - ICL_{NY})_{-1}$	0.10 (0.08)	0.09 (0.08)
$(Rshare_i)_{-1}$	−6.68 (15.94)	
$(Rratio_i - Rratio_{US})_{-1}$		−0.007 (0.006)
$(Debits_i - Debits_{US})_{-1}$	−0.18 (0.45)	−0.23 (0.41)
ρ		
D-h	0.476	0.402
R^2	.81	.82
Observations	93	93
Method	OLS	OLS

Notes: Standard errors are in parentheses. ρ is the coefficient of first-order autocorrelation. D-h is Durbin's h statistic. Method refers to the method used to estimate the regression: IV refers to the instrumental variable method; OLS to ordinary least squares.
***, **, and * indicate statistical significance at the .01, .05, and .10 levels (one-tail tests).

Table 4.2

Reserve Bank Discount Rate Policies
January 1924-February 1933. Dependent variable: $DR_i - DR_{NY}$

District:	Boston	Boston	Phila.	Phila.
Intercept	0.32 (0.66)	0.03 (0.02)	−0.38 (1.35)	0.25 (0.11)**
$(DR_i - DR_{NY})_{-1}$	0.25 (0.17)*	0.84 (0.05)***	0.13 (0.14)	0.17 (0.13)
$(CL_i - CL_{NY})_{-1}$	0.08 (0.09)	0.10 (0.09)	0.24 (0.13)**	0.28 (0.13)**
$(Rshare_i)_{-1}$	−2.21 (10.30)		11.08 (22.67)	
$(Rratio_i - Rratio_{US})_{-1}$		0.006 (0.003)		0.005 (0.010)
$(Debits_i - Debits_{US})_{-1}$	−0.46 (0.39)	0.03 (0.30)	0.34 (0.59)	0.33 (0.62)
ρ	−0.77 (0.06)***		−0.81 (0.06)***	−0.75 (0.07)***
D-h		1.058		
R^2	.73	.74	.80	.79
Observations	109	109	109	109
Method	IV	OLS	IV	IV
District:	Cleveland	Cleveland	Richmond	Richmond
Intercept	1.62 (0.91)*	0.02 (0.04)	0.34 (0.73)	0.17 (0.14)
$(DR_i - DR_{NY})_{-1}$	0.15 (0.14)	0.89 (0.04)***	0.57 (0.16)***	0.51 (0.15)***
$(CL_i - CL_{NY})_{-1}$	0.15 (0.09)**	0.07 (0.05)*	0.08 (0.08)	0.07 (0.08)
$(Rshare_i)_{-1}$	−18.02 (11.46)*		−6.97 (24.40)	
$(Rratio_i - Rratio_{US})_{-1}$		−0.023 (0.006)***		−0.000 (0.005)
$(Debits_i - Debits_{US})_{-1}$	−0.01 (0.51)	0.63 (0.35)**	0.42 (0.50)	0.41 (0.51)
ρ	−0.88 (0.05)***		−0.78 (0.06)***	−0.77 (0.06)***
D-h		1.448		
R^2	.85	.86	.85	.84
Observations	109	109	109	109
Method	IV	OLS	IV	IV

(*continued*)

Table 4.2, cont.

Reserve Bank Discount Rate Policies
January 1924-February 1933. Dependent variable: $DR_i - DR_{NY}$

District:	Atlanta	Atlanta	Chicago	Chicago
Intercept	0.33 (0.61)	0.03 (0.16)	1.35 (1.02)	0.35 (0.12)•••
$(DR_i - DR_{NY})_{-1}$	0.49 (0.14)•••	0.46 (0.13)•••	0.15 (0.13)	−0.10 (0.15)
$(CL_i - CL_{NY})_{-1}$	0.23 (0.11)••	0.25 (0.11)••	0.14 (0.11)	0.13 (0.11)
$(Rshare_i)_{-1}$	−11.05 (20.00)		−7.79 (6.87)	
$(Rratio_i - Rratio_{US})_{-1}$		0.000 (0.007)		−0.013 (0.008)••
$(Debits_i - Debits_{US})_{-1}$	−0.26 (0.47)	−0.32 (0.46)	−1.29 (0.61)	−1.01 (0.63)
ρ	−0.73 (0.07)•••	−0.77 (0.06)•••	−0.82 (0.06)•••	−0.81 (0.06)•••
D-h				
R^2	.84	.84	.80	.80
Observations	109	109	109	109
Method	IV	IV	IV	IV
District:	St. Louis	St. Louis	Minn.	Minn.
Intercept	0.78 (0.93)	0.29 (0.16)•	2.15 (0.86)••	0.19 (0.15)
$(DR_i - DR_{NY})_{-1}$	0.47 (0.26)••	0.34 (0.17)••	−0.07 (0.20)	0.37 (0.11)•••
$(CL_i - CL_{NY})_{-1}$	0.16 (0.11)•	0.19 (0.11)••	0.07 (0.11)	0.03 (0.11)
$(Rshare_i)_{-1}$	−18.77 (26.10)		−76.02 (37.10)••	
$(Rratio_i - Rratio_{US})_{-1}$		0.009 (0.005)		−0.018 (0.007)•••
$(Debits_i - Debits_{US})_{-1}$	−0.34 (0.44)	−0.42 (0.45)	−0.17 (0.36)	0.18 (0.36)
ρ	−0.86 (0.05)•••	−0.82 (0.06)•••	−0.90 (0.04)•••	−0.82 (0.06)•••
D-h				
R^2	.82	.82	.86	.87
Observations	109	109	109	109
Method	IV	IV	IV	IV

(*continued*)

Table 4.2, cont.

Reserve Bank Discount Rate Policies
January 1924-February 1933. Dependent variable: $DR_i - DR_{NY}$

District:	K. City	K. City	Dallas	Dallas
Intercept	1.39 (0.88)	−0.10 (0.12)	1.31 (0.70)*	−0.04 (0.13)
$(DR_i - DR_{NY})_{-1}$	0.40 (0.13)***	0.42 (0.10)***	0.37 (0.13)***	0.50 (0.10)***
$(CL_i - CL_{NY})_{-1}$	0.24 (0.11)**	0.27 (0.10)***	0.17 (0.09)**	0.28 (0.09)***
$(Rshare_i)_{-1}$	−35.33 (22.19)*		−44.56 (24.71)**	
$(Rratio_i - Rratio_{US})_{-1}$		−0.017 (0.006)***		−0.002 (0.006)
$(Debits_i - Debits_{US})_{-1}$	0.26 (0.61)	0.29 (0.56)	−0.58 (0.54)	−0.33 (0.59)
ρ	−0.72 (0.07)***	−0.75 (0.07)***	−0.70 (0.07)***	−0.62 (0.08)***
D-h				
R^2	.85	.87	.85	.83
Observations	109	109	109	109
Method	IV	IV	IV	IV

District:	San Francisco	San Francisco
Intercept	0.52 (0.50)	0.00 (0.04)
$(DR_i - DR_{NY})_{-1}$	0.84 (0.07)***	0.86 (0.07)***
$(CL_i - CL_{NY})_{-1}$	0.05 (0.08)	0.06 (0.07)
$(Rshare_i)_{-1}$	−6.86 (6.63)	
$(Rratio_i - Rratio_{US})_{-1}$		−0.008 (0.005)*
$(Debits_i - Debits_{US})_{-1}$	0.05 (0.42)	0.04 (0.41)
ρ		
D-h	1.084	1.107
R^2	.81	.82
Observations	109	109
Method	OLS	OLS

Notes: Standard errors are in parentheses. ρ is the coefficient of first-order autocorrelation. D-h is Durbin's h statistic. Method refers to the method used to estimate the regression: IV refers to the instrumental variable method; OLS to ordinary least squares.
***, **, and * indicate statistical significance at the .01, .05, and .10 levels (one-tail tests).

although statistically significant in just ten. This suggests that regional differences in market interest rates contributed somewhat to the lack of uniformity in discount rates.[22] An increase, for example, in the commercial-loan rate in a particular district relative to that in New York led the local Federal Reserve Bank to increase its discount rate relative to New York's discount rate.

The coefficient on the district reserve share is negative in the regressions of ten Reserve banks (of eleven possible), and it is statistically significant in seven. This supports the hypothesis that the Reserve Banks adjusted their discount rates in response to changes in their districts' reserve share. A decline in reserve share led to a discount-rate increase relative to the New York rate. Thus during the depression, when the reserve shares of many of the districts fell, the Reserve Banks outside New York apparently sought to limit reserve losses by increasing their discount rates relative to the New York rate.

The apparent response to changes in member-bank reserve share might in fact reflect the reaction of a Reserve Bank to changes in its own reserve position. In general, the variables $Rratio_i - Rratio_{US}$ and $Rshare_i$ were highly correlated.[23] I estimated a second regression for each district in which the latter variable was replaced by the former. In seven of these regressions the coefficient on $Rratio_i - Rratio_{US}$ is negative, although it is statistically significant in just three. While some of the Reserve Banks indicated that changes in this differential influenced their discount-rate setting, the econometric evidence is not particularly strong. Nevertheless, a decline in their reserve ratios, relative to the System's ratio, during the depression, probably contributed to the reluctance of some Reserve Banks to cut their discount rates.

---

[22] It is possible that regional differences in the commercial paper rate, or some other open-market rate, would be a more appropriate independent variable than the commercial-loan rate differential. Open-market rates are a closer measure of the opportunity cost of discount-window borrowing. And the replies of the Federal Reserve Banks to the Senate Banking Committee survey indicate also that the Banks responded to changes in open-market rates. Unfortunately, consistent data on open-market interest rates in each district are not available.

[23] From January 1924–September 1931, the correlation between these variables was positive and significant at the .10 level in eight of eleven districts outside New York.

The final independent variable, the difference between the percentage change in bank debits in district i and the percentage change in the nation as a whole, has a positive coefficient in just eleven (of a possible twenty-two) regressions, and is significant in only four. Differences in economic activity between the local district and the nation as a whole seem not to account for much of the absence of discount-rate uniformity. This is consistent with Eichengreen's model, in which central banks will be less sensitive to economic conditions when there is an absence of cooperation among them.

The regression results for January 1924–February 1933 are generally consistent with those for January 1924–September 1931. In addition to indicating persistence in the discount-rate differentials, they tend to support the hypothesis that market-rate differentials contributed to differences in discount rates. And, while admittedly weak, there is some evidence that the Reserve Banks sought to counter reserve flows and changes in their relative reserve ratios through adjustments in their discount rates. During the depression the member-bank reserve shares and reserve ratios of several of the districts declined, and Reserve Bank attempts to stem these declines resulted in an upward bias in discount rates. The resulting high discount rates outside New York discouraged member-bank borrowing. And the sharp decline in member-bank borrowing following the stock market crash caused much of the declines in Federal Reserve credit outstanding and in the money supply. Referring to the period from August 1929 to October 1930, Friedman and Schwartz (1963, pp. 340–41) write:

Ultimately then, it was the failure of the Reserve System to replace the decline in discounts by other credit outstanding that was responsible for the decline in the stock of money . . . Though the discount rate [of the Federal Reserve Bank of New York] fell absolutely, it probably rose relative to the relevant market interest rates. . . . Hence, discounting became less attractive.

If discounting "became less attractive" in the New York district as the depression progressed, it certainly was so in other districts. The differences between the discount rates of each Reserve Bank and the open-market rate on commercial paper in New York City in various months during the depression are listed in Table 4.3.[24] While generally exceeding discount rates in 1928 and 1929, market rates fell sharply relative to discount rates after the stock market crash. In January 1930, the discount rates of five Reserve Banks exceeded the commercial-paper rate. In July 1930 discount rates were higher in all but the Boston and New York districts, and in July 1931 only the discount rate of the Federal Reserve Bank of New York was below the commercial-paper rate. Market rates rose above most discount rates during the fourth quarter of 1931, despite discount-rate increases. But, in 1932 as the financial crisis subsided and market rates again fell, only New York and Chicago reduced their discount rates below 3.5%. And, by mid-1932, the discount rate of each Reserve Bank, including New York, was higher than the commercial-paper rate.

Why New York and Chicago failed to reduce their discount rates below 2.5 percent and the other Reserve banks failed to go below 3.5 percent remains a mystery. Perhaps they felt that under the circumstances rate reductions would do no good. . . . However, if this was a mistake it was minor as compared with the System's failure to buy more securities sooner in order to saturate banks with reserves in excess of legal requirements and even in excess of the amounts that banks hungry for liquidity would want to hold. (Chandler 1971, p. 208)

The reluctance to use open-market operations

As with discount-rate policy, there was considerable disagreement within the Federal Reserve System about the use of open-market operations. As described in Chapter 3, the proximate objective of open-market operations during economic downturns was monetary ease, which Fed officials gauged by the levels of member-bank borrowing and market interest rates. Since both were low during the depression, officials believed that large open-market purchases were unneeded. Indeed, some officials pressed for open-market sales, ar-

---

[24] As discussed in Chapter 3, the economic cost of borrowing from the Federal Reserve is the difference between the discount rate and cost of acquiring reserves in some other way, such as selling a security. Although commercial loan rates tended to be higher outside New York, this rate probably does not indicate best the cost of acquiring reserves. Because of correspondent links, it seems that the alternative interest rate would have been the market rate on short-term paper in New York City, regardless of where the borrowing bank was located.

Table 4.3

Discount Rates Minus Commercial Paper Interest Rate

Month

District	7/29	1/30	7/30	1/31	7/31	1/32	7/32
Boston	−1.00	−0.38	−0.22	−0.36	0.00	−0.38	1.00
New York	−1.00	−0.38	−0.75	−0.88	−0.50	−0.38	0.00
Philadelphia	−1.00	−0.14	0.28	0.62	1.00	−0.38	1.00
Cleveland	−1.00	0.12	0.25	0.12	0.50	−0.38	1.00
Richmond	−1.00	0.12	0.52	0.62	1.00	0.01	1.00
Atlanta	−1.00	−0.38	0.43	0.27	1.00	−0.38	1.00
Chicago	−1.00	−0.38	0.25	0.27	0.50	−0.38	0.00
St. Louis	−1.00	0.12	0.75	0.23	0.50	−0.38	1.00
Minneapolis	−1.00	0.12	0.75	0.62	1.50	−0.38	1.00
Kansas City	−1.00	−0.38	0.75	0.62	1.00	−0.38	1.00
Dallas	−1.00	0.12	0.75	0.62	1.00	0.06	1.00
San Francisco	−1.00	−0.38	0.75	0.25	0.50	−0.38	1.00

Source: Board of Governors of the Federal Reserve System (1943: 441, 450-51).

guing that monetary ease had actually interfered with economic recovery. These officials believed that open-market purchases in 1924 and 1927 had fueled stock market speculation and thus contributed to the severity of the eventual crash and depression. They were concerned that purchases would reignite speculation and delay the process of liquidation which they saw as necessary before economic recovery could begin.

George Harrison, who became Governor of the Federal Reserve Bank of New York following the death of Benjamin Strong, and Eugene Black, Governor of the Federal Reserve Bank of Atlanta, were the only Reserve Bank governors who advocated significant open-market purchases during the depression. Most of the other members of the Open Market Committee argued that monetary conditions were sufficiently easy, and a few, such as James McDougal of the Chicago Fed, pressed for open-market sales. These officials warned against a policy of "artificial" ease, and pressed for sales to "soak up" excess money and hasten liquidation of speculative loans.[25] They never succeeded in winning approval of sales, but they did prevent substantial purchases before 1932.

The 1931 Senate Banking Committee hearings revealed many of the disagreements within the Reserve System about the conduct of monetary policy. Of principal concern was the relationship between Federal Reserve policies during the 1920s and the economic problems of the 1930s.

Carter Glass chaired the hearings, and his opinion of Fed behavior during the 1920s is clear from their transcript. Glass was particularly incensed about the unwillingness of the Federal Reserve Bank of New York to refuse borrowing privileges to member banks holding stock market loans. In response to testimony by George Harrison that the Reserve Banks could not control the use of reserves provided through the discount window, Glass reacted sharply:

The plain intent of the proponents of this [the Federal Reserve] act was to remove the assets of the Federal reserve banking system as far away from stock speculative activities and purposes as it was possible. . . . It is the business of the Federal reserve bank to know what the borrowing [bank] is doing and for what purpose it is doing it. (United States Senate 1931, pp. 53–55)

Glass was also critical of the open-market purchases initiated by Benjamin Strong during the 1920s, particularly those in 1927. Adolph Miller explained that the funds provided by these purchases had fueled stock market speculation, which he argued had contributed to the severity of the crash and subsequent depression:

It was the greatest and boldest operation ever undertaken by the Federal reserve system, and, in my judgement, resulted in one of the most costly errors committed by it or any banking system in the last 75 years. I am inclined to think that a different policy at that time would have left us with a different condition at this time. . . . That was a time of business recession.

---

[25] For example, in January 1931 McDougal "proposed that the System sell some of its government securities . . . in order to eliminate 'sloppiness' in the money market" (Chandler 1971, p. 135). See Friedman and Schwartz (1963, pp. 362–91), Chandler (1971, Ch. 9 and 10) and Epstein and Ferguson (1984) for further analysis of disagreements within the Reserve System over open-market policy during the depression.

Business could not use and was not asking for increased money at that time. (ibid., p. 134)

Glass agreed that the purchases had been a mistake: "If there are no rediscounts, what will the Federal reserve banks do with their accumulated funds? . . . Except to use their resources in the open market as was disastrously done? (ibid., p. 138)"

Glass' opposition to centralized control of monetary policy was strengthened by his strong feelings about the 1927 purchases, and he asked Miller about the influence of the "average" Federal Reserve Bank on open-market policy. Miller replied:

I should say that until a comparatively recent date, the influence of . . . the [non-New York] banks in the . . . system was trifling. But I think the miscarriage of the 1927 adventure . . . has served to make the . . . outside banks . . . more solicitous, and it is largely due to their feeling that the open-market committee has changed its character and its size. (ibid: 140)[26]

The exchange between Glass and Miller indicate their anti-New York sentiments.[27] To the extent that Miller's views were shared by other System officials, the shift of power away from New York probably reduced the Fed's willingness to use open-market operations during the depression.

Further criticism of the Fed's policies during the 1920s is found in the answers of the Reserve Banks to the Banking Committee survey. One question asked, "Viewed in light of subsequent events, what policies should the Federal Reserve Banks have followed in the purchase of United States securities in 1924 and 1927?" The responses are summarized well by the Boston Fed's answer: "Both of these purchase operations appear to have been successful. The principal criticism might be with the tardy reversal in the latter part of 1927" (ibid., p. 815). Even New York officials believed that the 1924 and

---

[26] Miller was referring to the formation of the Open Market Policy Conference in March 1930, in which the governors of all twelve Reserve Banks were members. This replaced the Open Market Investment Committee, in which the governors of just five Banks were members.

[27] Apparently there was considerable antagonism between Miller and Benjamin Strong (Chandler 1958, pp. 44–45). Glass and Strong disagreed sharply about policy in 1919–20, when Glass was Treasury secretary, and throughout the 1920s Glass spoke against Strong's accumulation of power (ibid., pp. 163–64, 449–50; Wicker 1966a, pp. 37–38).

1927 purchases had been too large; "It is our opinion that purchases of securities in both 1924 and 1927 were most helpful and desirable. . . . [However] the 1924 purchases were carried further than now appears to have been desirable." The reply also states that more substantial open-market sales and discount-rate increases should have been made in 1928 (ibid., p. 817).

Benjamin Strong also seems to have believed that the Fed had purchased too heavily in 1924. Testifying before the House Committee on Banking and Currency in 1926, he stated: "I think myself, if it were to be done over again, we might have stopped a month earlier or even 60 days earlier. We might have bought $50,000,000 or even $100,000,000 less, but there is no mathematical formula that will tell you where to stop or to begin" (United States House of Representatives 1926, p. 336). And W. Randolph Burgess (1946 [1927], p. 289), wrote later that "perhaps less of an easy money policy in 1927 would now appear to . . . have been desirable."

All of the Reserve Banks agreed that the 1924 and 1927 purchases had been effective in easing credit. But a few questioned whether any open-market purchases should have been made in those years, and all agreed that there had been insufficient open-market sales in 1928. The Chicago Reserve Bank responded that the System had bought too heavily in 1924, and "in 1927 the danger of putting money into the market was greater than in 1924 as speculation was well under way, and it would now appear that the objects which were accomplished at that time were more than offset by the loss of control of the money market situation" (United States Senate 1931, p. 815). The Philadelphia Bank questioned whether Federal Reserve credit should ever be extended except at the initiative of member banks, and the Richmond Fed replied, "we think United States securities should not have been purchased in these periods, and the aim should have been to decrease rather than augment the total supply of Federal reserve credit" (ibid., p. 817). Within the Reserve System there remained considerable acceptance of the Real Bills view that the supply of credit should decline during recessions, because lacking "productive" outlets an excess supply would generate speculation or inflation.

The fear of speculation and inflation influenced policy during the 1920s, and affected it no less during the 1930s. Frederic Curtis, Chairman of the Federal Reserve Bank of Boston, opposed open-market purchases "on the ground that they were likely to feed the stock market rather than the bond market" (Friedman and Schwartz 1963, p. 373). And James McDougal argued that even if purchases did not lead to stock market speculation, they might fuel speculation "in some other direction" (ibid., p. 371).

The fear of speculation was not confined to the Federal Reserve. The stock market recovered a bit in early 1930, and that, according to Harris (1933, p. 622), was enough to prevent the Fed from pursuing expansionary policies: "The hesitation on the part of reserve authorities can be easily condoned. The incipient stock market boom, which set in in the spring of 1930, necessarily was followed by hesitation."[28] Others criticized the Fed for failing to pursue policies designed to squeeze excess liquidity out of the system. Hayek (1932, p. 130), for example, wrote:

It is a fact that the present crisis is marked by the first attempt on a large scale to revive the economy immediately after the sudden reversal of the upswing, by a systematic policy of lowering the interest rate accompanied by all other possible measures for preventing the normal process of liquidation, and that as a result the depression has assumed more devastating forms and lasted longer than ever before. . . . It is quite probable that we would have been over the want long ago and that the fall in prices would never have assumed such disastrous proportions, if the process of liquidation had been allowed to take its course after the crisis of 1929.

Hayek's view that Federal Reserve policy had been too easy was shared by a number of System officials. But even those not of this opinion tended to view open-market operations with skepticism, and believed that open-market purchases in the 1920s had fueled stock market speculation. This perception strengthened the position of Miller, McDougal, George Norris (Governor of the Philadelphia

---

[28] The "boom" to which Harris referred was reflected in an increase in the Standard and Poor's common stock index from 159.6 in November 1929 to 191.1 in April 1930. The index had peaked at 237.8 in September 1929 (1935–39 = 100) (Board of Governors of the Federal Reserve System 1943, p. 481).

Fed), and John Calkins (Governor of the San Francisco Fed) who adamantly opposed open-market purchases.

Under pressure from Congress and major commercial banks, the Fed did buy some $1 billion of government securities in the second quarter of 1932. Several Fed officials remained skeptical, however. When purchases were discussed at a meeting of the Open Market Policy Conference on February 24, 1932 there was little agreement about the efficacy of open-market operations, and a number of governors questioned whether purchases would benefit banks throughout the country or simply cause excess reserves to pile up in financial centers (Chandler 1971, p. 193). Harris (1933, pp. 620–21) had the same concern: "the surplus cash created as a result of open market operations may find its way neither to banks heavily in debt nor to communities especially in need of the added stimulus."

While these doubts focused on the regional dispersion of reserves generated by purchases, the underlying concern was on the ultimate use of the reserves provided. The perceived connection between System purchases and stock market activity in the 1920s reflected a belief that reserves generated by the purchases had flowed to Wall Street rather than been dispersed evenly throughout the country. And, at least some officials believed that another purchase program would cause similar speculative excesses without leading to a general economic recovery.

The regional impact of open-market operations

Benjamin Strong explained to the Governors Conference in November 1923 how open-market operations made solely in New York City affected banking conditions throughout the country:

The first result of buying by Reserve Banks . . . is to bring about a very sharp reduction in the borrowings of member banks from the Reserve Banks in New York, first, and in Philadelphia, Boston, and Cleveland. The proceeds of the purchases will drift at once to the money centers, and as discounts are repaid, it eases money in three or four principal money markets . . . and the effect of easier money at the money centers spreads throughout the whole country, and the banks in the money centers have a surplus to loan. (Quoted in Chandler 1958, p. 239)

Fed officials observed that open-market operations, in conjunction with gold flows and other changes in nonborrowed reserves, led to opposite changes in member-bank borrowing. And through their effect on member-bank borrowing, officials believed that open-market operations influenced the cost and availability of credit.

Beginning in 1923, the open-market operations of the individual Reserve Banks were coordinated by the Open Market Investment Committee and were carried out in New York City. Prior to the stock market crash the Committee purchased securities in 1924, 1926, and 1927, and sold in 1925, 1926, and 1928–29. Figure 4.5 plots the Fed's government security holdings from January 1924–December 1929. Also plotted are the nonborrowed reserves of member banks in the New York district, and in all other districts combined. A correspondence between the System's open-market operations and changes in nonborrowed reserves, both within New York and outside, is evident.

The Fed purchased some $500 million of securities in 1924. Combined with gold inflows of $200 million, nonborrowed reserves increased by about $700 million. Consistent with Strong's description of the regional impact of open-market operations, throughout the country nonborrowed reserves rose, while member-bank borrowing and interest rates fell. The commercial-paper rate in New York City declined from 4.88% in January 1924 to a low of 3.13% in September–October, and closed the year at 3.63%. The rates on other short-term rates fell similarly, as did commercial-loan rates in each Federal Reserve district city (Table 4.4).

The Fed sold securities in 1925, and again the correlation between the Fed's operations and changes in nonborrowed reserves both in New York and outside is clear. Open-market purchases in 1927 led to an increase in nonborrowed reserves, and sales in 1928 and early 1929 obviously were correlated with a reduction in nonborrowed reserves. In 1928 there was a distinct change in the regional distribution of nonborrowed reserves, however, with New York's share

Table 4.4

Commercial Loan Interest Rates

Federal Reserve Bank Cities

1924

City	High (month)		Low (month)	
Boston	5%	(Jan.)	4%	(Nov.)
New York	5 - 5.5	(Jan.)	3.5 - 6	(Nov.)
Philadelphia	5.5	(Jan.)	4 - 4.5	(Sep.)
Cleveland	6	(Jan.)	5 - 6	(June)
Richmond	6	(Jan.)	5 - 5.5	(Sep.)
Atlanta	5.5	(Jan.)	4.5 - 6	(June)
Chicago	5 - 6	(Jan.)	4 - 4.8	(Aug.)
St. Louis	5.5	(Jan.)	3.5 - 5	(Oct.)
Minneapolis	5.5	(Jan.)	4.5	(Nov.)
Kansas City	6	(Jan.)	5 - 6	(Aug.)
Dallas	6	(Jan.)	4 - 6	(Oct.)
San Francisco	6	(Apr.)	4.5 - 5	(Oct.)

Notes:

The interest rates are for 4 to 6 month prime commercial loans, and are as of mid-month.

The month in which the particular rate (or spread) first appeared is given in parentheses.

Source: Federal Reserve Board, Annual Report (1925: 200-01).

rising relative to the other districts'. There was not a similar increase in New York's share of total member-bank reserves until the end of 1928, however. New York's shares of both nonborrowed and total reserves rose markedly in 1929 (except for a brief, but dramatic, one month decline in July 1929). New York's reserve shares declined temporarily in the wake of the stock market crash with the liquidation of security loans. But, beginning in 1930, New York's reserve shares resumed climbing again.

The national stock of bank reserves is determined largely by the

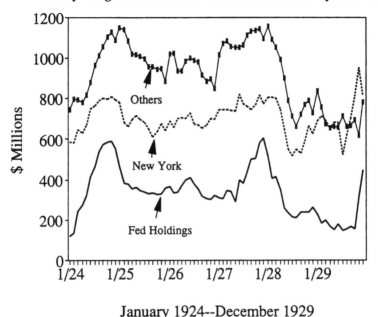

January 1924--December 1929

Figure 4.5. Nonborrowed reserves and Federal Reserve Government Security holdings, January 1924–December 1929.

supply provided by the Federal Reserve System.[29] However the regional distribution of reserves is determined by demand. Flows of reserves to New York in 1928 and 1929 thwarted the Fed's attempt to control the supply of funds invested in stock market loans. Similarly, during the depression bank reserves flowed mainly to large New York and Chicago banks, and by 1932 these banks had accumulated substantial excess reserves. The inability to target the flow of

---

[29] More precisely, during the 1920s and early 1930s the Fed controlled the stock of nonborrowed reserves, with the quantity of total reserves also a function of member-bank demands for borrowed reserves. In these years borrowed reserves comprised a much larger component of total reserves than they have since World War II. Had the Fed set its discount rate above market rates, i.e., made it a penalty rate, or if it had controlled borrowing by some other means, then the Fed would have controlled total reserves. However, the discount rate was not a penalty rate throughout much of the period, and the System did not fix the supply of borrowed reserves. Hence, to a degree, the stock of reserves was determined by demand, with member-bank borrowing adjusting as necessary to absorb changes in nonborrowed reserves.

reserves generated by open-market sales in 1928 and 1929, or by
what few purchases were made following the crash, likely contributed to the reluctance of Fed officials to make large-scale purchases before 1932, and then to the abandonment of that program.

Reserve dispersion during the depression

Figure 4.6 plots the Fed's government security holdings and the
stocks of nonborrowed reserves in New York and outside districts
from January 1928–August 1931. The increase in New York's reserve share prior to the stock market crash is clear, as is the decline
in that share following the crash. In the wake of the crash, the
Reserve System bought some $300 million of securities. And from
January 1930–August 1931 the Fed accumulated an additional $200
million of securities. While New York's share of reserves rose some-

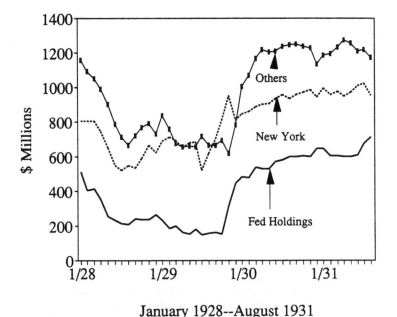

January 1928--August 1931

Figure 4.6. Nonborrowed reserves and Federal Reserve Government Security holdings, January 1928–August 1931.

what in these months, the increase was not particularly dramatic. Figure 4.7 plots the Fed's security holdings and nonborrowed reserves from January 1930–February 1933. Beginning in mid-1931, and accelerating in late September, the national stock of nonborrowed reserves fell sharply. One effect of Britain's abandonment of the gold standard was to cause foreigners to draw down their deposits in American banks, many of which were held in New York City banks. However, the New York district's share of nonborrowed reserves rose dramatically (although its share of total reserves did not) as the panic enveloped the country and depositors shifted funds to New York banks, which were still perceived as safer. New York's share of nonborrowed reserves fell somewhat after the crisis had passed, but in 1932 remained well above its precrisis level. Moreover, the New York share of total reserves also increased sharply in 1932. New York City and Chicago banks accumulated substantial

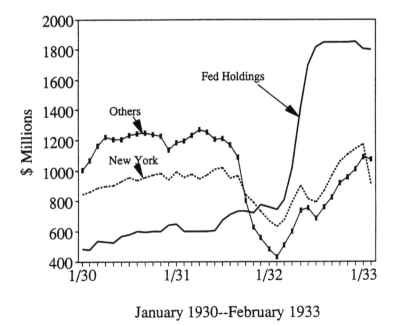

January 1930--February 1933

Figure 4.7. Nonborrowed reserves and Federal Reserve Government Security holdings, January 1930–February 1933.

excess reserves in 1932, while banks in smaller cities and rural areas remained heavily in debt to the Reserve Banks. This led contemporaries, and some recent studies to argue that "these figures cast doubt on the efficacy of open-market operations in relieving the squeeze on the economy outside of financial markets" (Kindleberger [1973] 1968, pp. 185–87).

From February–August 1932, member bank nonborrowed reserves rose by $563 million. Although the Fed bought $1107 million of government securities during this period, its holdings of bankers acceptances fell by $114 million. Gold outflows totaling $345 million and an increase in currency outstanding of $92 million further offset the impact of the Fed's purchases on bank reserves. The changes in nonborrowed, borrowed, and total member-bank reserves in each Federal Reserve district during these months are presented in Table 4.5. Forty-one percent of the increase in non-borrowed reserves accumulated in the New York district, which was somewhat less than the percentage of all U.S. nonborrowed reserves held by New York district banks. However, 89% of the national increase in total reserves went to New York district banks. In most districts member-bank borrowing declined by about as much as nonborrowed reserves rose, and consequently total reserves changed little. The 3.5% discount rates maintained by all of the Reserve Banks, except New York and Chicago, during 1932 were definitely "penalty" rates. Even the 2.5% rates of the New York and Chicago Banks were well above market interest rates (see Table 4.3).[30] It is not surprising that banks used the increase in nonborrowed reserves to reduce their discount loans.

Because New York City banks were entirely out of debt by April 1932, the flow of nonborrowed reserves to those banks produced an increase in their total reserves. Further purchases would have been necessary to build up total reserves in all districts, however, particularly among Country member banks. In February 1932, Central Reserve City banks held just $31 million of borrowed reserves (4%

---

[30] The market rate on commercial paper declined from 3.88 to 1.5% during 1932, and was below 3.5% after April. The rate on bankers' acceptances fell from 2.88 to 0.38% in 1932 (Board of Governors of the Federal Reserve System 1943, pp. 451).

Table 4.5

District Reserve Flows

February–August 1932

District	Non-Borrowed		Borrowed		Total	
Boston	32.2	(.06)	−20.7	(.05)	11.5	(.07)
New York	232.8	(.41)	−85.8	(.22)	147.0	(.89)
Philadelphia	55.3	(.10)	−56.8	(.14)	−1.5	(−.01)
Cleveland	86.5	(.15)	−86.2	(.22)	0.3	(.00)
Richmond	7.0	(.01)	−8.7	(.02)	−1.7	(−.01)
Atlanta	10.2	(.02)	−15.4	(.04)	−5.2	(−.03)
Chicago	83.4	(.15)	−46.7	(.12)	36.7	(.22)
St. Louis	5.2	(.01)	−9.6	(.02)	−4.4	(−.03)
Minneapolis	−1.9	(−.00)	−0.6	(.00)	−2.5	(−.01)
Kansas City	15.3	(.03)	−17.5	(.04)	−2.2	(−.02)
Dallas	−7.9	(−.01)	1.7	(−.00)	−6.2	(−.04)
San Francisco	43.8	(.08)	−51.0	(.13)	−7.2	(−.04)

Notes:

Reserves data are in $ million. The number in parentheses is the district's share of the reserve flow. Source: Federal Reserve Board Annual Report (1932: 53).

of their total reserves), while Reserve City banks held $404 million (66% of their total reserves), and Country member banks held $399 million (84% of their total reserves). In August 1932, Central Reserve City banks had borrowings of just $6 million (less than 1% of their total reserves), Reserve City banks had borrowings of $136 million (22% of their total reserves), and Country banks had borrowings of $308 million (69% of their total reserves) (Board of Governors of the Federal Reserve System 1943, pp. 397–99). Because banks still held $450 million of borrowed reserves when the Fed ended its purchases in August 1932, further purchases would have been necessary to produce increases in total reserves in all districts.

Despite the high discount rates, member banks did not use the entire increase in nonborrowed reserves to reduce their borrowings.

While open-market operations were conducted entirely in New York City, the Federal Reserve noted that Treasury disbursements and advances by the Reconstruction Finance Corporation had dispersed funds throughout the country:

> Funds acquired in this manner by the interior, not being employed locally, subsequently found their way back to New York and other financial centers through the redeposit of funds by outside banks with their city correspondents. . . . The figures indicate that the outside banks have a large volume of idle funds held on deposit with city banks whence they can be withdrawn on demand when the occasion arises. (Federal Reserve *Bulletin* February 1933, pp. 60–61)

The bulk of the increase in the correspondent balances of Country member banks occurred after the Fed had terminated its purchase program. For comparison, on September 29, 1931, Country member banks held correspondent balances of $787 million in domestic banks. On December 31, 1931 the figure was $685 million. On June 30, 1932 it was $671 million, and on December 31,1932 it was $767 million (Board of Governors of the Federal Reserve System 1943, p. 98). The increase in correspondent balances of this class of banks during 1932 was just $82 million, and most of the increase came after June 30. But, regardless of whether banks preferred to use non-borrowed reserve increases to reduce their borrowings from the Reserve Banks or to accumulate correspondent balances, it seems clear that further purchases were needed to satisfy bank demands for liquidity and to encourage new lending.[31]

It is not clear why the Fed discontinued its purchase program. Epstein and Ferguson (1984, pp. 969–72) argue that major banks pressured the Fed to discontinue because falling interest rates had reduced their profits. The System's view that the reserves created by the operations were "idle" funds, lacking a useful outlet undoubtedly

---

[31] Wicker (1966a, p. 180) suggests that banks may have preferred to accumulate some correspondent balances rather than use all of the increase in nonborrowed reserves to reduce their borrowings, despite the high discount rates, because "their supposed reluctance to remain indebted to the Federal Reserve banks was more than offset by their desire for immediate, quick liquidity." Thus, to an extent banks were willing to pay the Fed's high discount rate in order to hold some correspondent balances because of their extreme liquidity.

also contributed to the decision. A letter from James McDougal to George Harrison on July 9, 1932 probably describes the reasons accurately:

We are of the opinion that no additional purchases should be made by the System merely for the purpose of increasing the amount of member bank excess reserves. . . . We believe that the additional purchases made were much too large and have resulted in creating abnormally low rates for short-term U.S. government securities. (Quoted in Chandler 1971, p. 201)

The Fed made no purchases during 1932 after August. In fact, the Open Market Committee discussed selling securities. Fed officials believed that money was exceptionally easy, as indicated by low interest rates and the buildup of excess reserves. And most seem to have believed that the open-market purchase experiment had failed.

Summary

Building upon the work of Friedman and Schwartz (1963) and Chandler (1971), this chapter examines the nature of disagreements within the Federal Reserve during the depression, and describes how those disagreements affected System policy. The reluctance of a majority of Fed officials to support open-market purchases stemmed from a fundamental Real Bills view that the supply of credit should contract during recessions, reinforced by a perception that purchases made in 1924 and 1927 had fueled stock market speculation, and as a consequence worsened the inevitable crash and depression. It was feared that extensive purchases during the depression would reignite speculation without stimulating economic recovery.

While the Fed's open-market policy during the depression was anemic, outside of New York, Reserve Bank discount policy was in fact contractionary. Only the New York Fed matched declines in market rates with discount-rate cuts, and then only until October 1931. Previous studies have not focused on differences in the discount policies of the Reserve Banks, implicitly ascribing the relatively high discount rates outside of New York to the general conservatism and lack of understanding of officials in those Banks. Friedman and Schwartz (1963) and Epstein and Ferguson (1984) allude to the failure of the Reserve Banks to cooperate during the depression. This chapter emphasizes further how a lack of cooperation affected discount rates. The Reserve Banks competed with one another for reserves, and attempted to stem reserve outflows through discount rate increases. This competition imparted an upward bias on discount rates during the depression, which contributed to the decline in money supply, and surely exacerbated the Great Depression.

5. Conclusion

The failures of Federal Reserve policy making during the Great Depression cannot be attributed to a single cause. Flaws in the System's organization, goals, and methods all contributed to its mistakes. The System's decentralized organization slowed the Fed's response to crises and made consensus difficult to achieve. Its goal of maintaining the convertibility of the dollar into gold caused the Fed to take deflationary actions in the midst of the depression. And the failure of policy makers to interpret monetary conditions correctly caused them to believe that money and credit were plentiful while the banking system and money supply were collapsing.

In their *Monetary History of the United States*, Friedman and Schwartz (1963) argue that under the leadership of Benjamin Strong, Governor of the Federal Reserve Bank of New York, policies were developed that successfully limited fluctuations in economic activity. But Strong's death in 1928 and a subsequent reorganization of the Open Market Committee redistributed authority to officials who lacked the knowledge and experience to continue Strong's policies. Consequently, there was a dramatic change in Federal Reserve responsiveness to economic conditions. According to Friedman and Schwartz (1963, pp. 411–14), Strong would have prevented reorganization of the Open Market Committee, and his experience as an officer of Bankers Trust Company during the Panic of 1907 foretold that he would have reacted vigorously to the banking panic in 1930. But, perhaps most importantly, Friedman and Schwartz contend that officials of the Federal Reserve Bank of New York would have pursued appropriate policies, despite Strong's death, had they retained the degree of authority held by Strong.

I conclude, however, that Federal Reserve policy during the de-

113

pression was largely a continuation of previous policy. It is true that officials of the Federal Reserve Bank of New York occasionally advocated more aggressive countercyclical actions than were accepted by the rest of the System. But for two reasons Strong's death and the reorganization of the Open Market Committee probably had less effect on policy than Friedman and Schwartz contend. First, it is unclear whether Strong could have prevented the Committee's reorganization or some other diminution of his authority. A number of Fed officials believed that overly expansionary policy during the 1920s – Strong's policy – had contributed to stock market speculation and the subsequent depression. In particular, they blamed the open-market purchases of 1924 and 1927 for fueling speculation because they had come "when business could not use and was not asking for increased money" (Adolph Miller in United States Senate 1931, p. 134). Even one of the most vigorous proponents of open-market purchases during the depression, W. Randolph Burgess ([1927] 1946, p. 289), wrote later that policy had been too easy in 1927, and Strong himself testified in 1926 that it might have been appropriate to buy fewer securities in 1924 (United States House of Representatives 1926, p. 336). During the depression a number of Reserve Bank governors were concerned that purchases would reignite speculation and interfere with economic recovery. Given the prevalence of the opinion that earlier actions had contributed to the System's current predicament, it seems likely that Strong would have had difficulty finding support for significant open-market purchases during the depression.

A second reason to doubt the importance of Strong's death was that although the Fed was intent on limiting economic fluctuations during the 1920s, as the evidence presented in Chapter 2 indicates, the policy strategy designed by Strong was not directed at control of the money supply. Rather, the Fed had a "money market" or "reserve position" strategy not unlike those criticized by monetarists during the 1950s, 60s, and 70s. Officials used the level of member-bank borrowing to determine the volume of open-market operations necessary to achieve their ultimate goals. The Fed followed the simple rule that heavy borrowing indicated tight money and little borrowing indicated monetary ease. Thus, during a recession, if borrowing was relatively high the Fed would purchase a comparatively large quantity of securities. But, if member-bank borrowing was low, as it was in the early 1930s, the Fed bought few securities because it appeared that the proximate objective of purchases – monetary ease – had already been achieved. The Fed seems to have employed this strategy consistently from 1924 to 1933.

The Fed's use of member-bank borrowing as a policy guide resulted in procyclical changes in the supply of money. Indeed, this strategy permitted greater declines in the money supply during severe recessions than during minor ones. The econometric evidence in Chapter 3 indicates that member-bank borrowing was positively related to economic activity. During recessions member-bank borrowing fell in part because of declining loan demand. Thus, in a severe recession, loan demand, and hence member-bank borrowing, would decline significantly. Because officials interpreted little borrowing as a sign of monetary ease, the Fed responded *less* vigorously the *worse* the economic contraction. The use of member-bank borrowing as an indicator was particularly inappropriate during the depression because of instability in borrowed-reserve demand. Banking panics made banks cautious and less willing to borrow reserves since borrowing might signal weakness to depositors. Insufficient collateral also may have constrained the borrowing of some banks. The Fed seems to have been largely unaware of the shift and continued to interpret little borrowing as a sign of exceptional monetary ease.

The Great Depression caused considerable debate about the role of monetary policy, both within and outside the Federal Reserve System, and the views of Fed officials diverged widely. At one extreme, James McDougal, Governor of the Federal Reserve Bank of Chicago, among others, argued that the Fed should not interfere with natural economic forces by maintaining "artificially" easy monetary conditions. McDougal opposed open-market purchases, and occasionally advocated selling securities to soak up excess liquidity. At the other extreme, George Harrison and other officials of the Federal Reserve Bank of New York argued for providing sufficient reserves to keep money-center banks out of debt and interest rates low, proximate goals consistent with those suggested by Strong during the 1920s. In essence, Harrison and McDougal differed about the efficacy of monetary ease in promoting economic recovery.[1] They did, however, agree that the prevailing low market-interest rates, lack of significant borrowing by member banks, and growth of excess reserves signaled that money was exceptionally plentiful and inexpensive.[2]

While monetary policy during the depression was largely a continuation of previous policy, it is impossible to dismiss as unimportant the decentralized organization of the Reserve System or the changes in authority within the system at the onset of the depression. The weakness of the Federal Reserve Board and the legal freedom of the Reserve Banks to act independently made it difficult to formulate a national monetary policy or to respond quickly and decisively to crises. The decentralized structure fostered divergent discount-rate policies among the Reserve Banks, which became particularly evident during the depression when many of the Banks kept their rates high while the New York Fed brought its rate down quickly. This study indicates that competition for reserves and a lack of cooperation among the Banks contributed to this upward bias in discount rates. Had there been more centralized authority over rates, or had the Banks cooperated effectively, discount rates would likely have been set lower, thereby lessening the declines in member-bank borrowing and the money supply.

---

[1] Chandler (1971, pp. 117–23) refers to those with Harrison's view as the "accommodationists" and to those with McDougal's view as the "liquidationists."

[2] Meltzer (1976, pp. 467–68) argues similarly: "On a few occasions [some official] questioned the policy. The questioners were never able to alter the interpretation that low rates and little borrowing by member banks showed that policy was easy. The principal errors made by the Federal Reserve in the early thirties resulted from the reliance on the level of market rates of interest and member bank borrowing to indicate ease and restraint." Of course, this view is not shared by Friedman and Schwartz (1963) who believe that New York officials did interpret monetary conditions correctly (see also Schwartz 1981, p. 42). While the evidence is mixed, if they are correct then the institutional changes that they cite as *causing* a change in regime may in fact have *prevented* a change by locking the Fed into the simple reserve position strategy that it had employed in prior years. That is, because New York officials had lost authority they were unable to bring about a change in policy strategy. Monetary policy during the depression was largely a continuation of the strategy developed during the 1920s, and without its abandonment, some monetary contraction was inevitable.

All Federal Reserve officials desired an end to the depression. They differed to some extent on how to achieve that objective, but there were some things upon which they did agree. One was the idea that little member-bank borrowing signaled monetary ease. Another was the necessity of maintaining the gold standard. Defense of the gold standard was the priority of monetary policy in the fourth quarter of 1931 and again in early 1933. In these months Fed officials were willing to discard monetary ease as their proximate objective to maintain the gold standard. Their actions to defend gold caused a rapid decline in the money supply that further deepened the depression. As in 1921, Fed officials demonstrated their willingness to defend the convertibility of the dollar, regardless of the existing level of economic activity.

Federal Reserve behavior during the depression was thus largely consistent with earlier policies. The Fed desired to limit the depression, and sought monetary ease to achieve that goal. Unfortunately, the indicators that it used to judge monetary ease were inaccurate, and policy was in fact contractionary. While Benjamin Strong's death and reorganization of the Open Market Committee undoubtedly imparted some further contractionary bias to policy, there was no fundamental alteration of Fed strategy. And when the Fed temporarily abandoned monetary ease and domestic economic stability as its immediate policy goals in late 1931, it replaced them with defense of the gold standard, an even more traditional pillar of monetary policy.

Appendix: Variable definitions and data sources

For convenience, references to Board of Governors of the Federal Reserve System (1943) are noted as BMS (for *Banking and Monetary Statistics*).

AIP	Index of Industrial Production (seasonally adjusted). Federal Reserve Board, *Annual Report* (1937, pp. 175–77).
B	Member bank borrowing (discount loans). BMS, pp. 169–78 (weekly reporting member banks in New York City); Federal Reserve Board, *Annual Report* (various issues) (member banks in each Federal Reserve district).
BR	Acceptance buying rate (61–90 day), Federal Reserve Bank of New York. BMS, pp. 444–45.
C	Currency stock. BMS, pp. 370–71.
Debits	Debits to deposit accounts. BMS, pp. 234–35 (New York City); Federal Reserve Board, *Annual Report* (various issues) (for each Federal Reserve district).
DR	Discount rate, Federal Reserve Bank of New York. BMS, pp. 440–41.
Fail	Suspensions of all U.S. commercial banks. Federal Reserve Board, *Bulletin* (September 1937, p. 907).
G	Monetary gold stock. BMS, pp. 370–71.
GS	Federal Reserve System holdings of government securities. BMS, pp. 370–71.
I	Commercial paper (4–6 month) interest rate. BMS, pp. 450–51.
ICL	Commercial loan interest rate. Federal Reserve Board, *Annual Report* (various issues).

IUK   Bankers acceptance rate (90 day) in London. BMS, pp. 656–58.

IUS   Bankers acceptance rate (90 day) in New York. BMS, pp. 450–51.

MemFail Suspensions of Federal Reserve member banks. Federal Reserve Board, *Bulletin* (September 1937, p. 907).

PRI   All commodities price index. Federal Reserve Board, *Bulletin* (various issues).

R^n Nonborrowed reserves of member banks. BMS, pp. 169–78 (weekly reporting banks in New York City); Federal Reserve Board, *Annual Report* (various issues) (New York district member banks).

Rratio   Federal Reserve Bank reserve ratio. Federal Reserve Board, *Annual Report* (various issues).

Rshare   Ratio of the total reserves of all member banks in a Federal Reserve district to the total reserves of all U.S. member banks. Federal Reserve Board, *Annual Report* (various issues).

STK   Standard and Poor's index of common stock prices. BMS, pp. 480–81.

Wage   Industrial real hourly wage rate. Beney (1936, pp. 45–47).

References

Aigner, D. J., and Bryan, W. R. 1968. "The Determinants of Member Bank Borrowing: A Critique." *Journal of Finance* 23 (December): 832–37.

Alston, L. J., Grove, W. A., and Wheelock, D. C. 1991. "Why Do Banks Fail? Evidence from the 1920s." Unpublished manuscript.

Beney, M. A. 1936. *Wages, Hours and Employment in the United States 1914–1936.* New York: National Industrial Conference Board.

Bernanke, B. S. 1983. "Nonmonetary Effects of the Financial Crises in the Propagation of the Great Depression." *American Economic Review* 73 (June): 257–76.

Board of Governors of the Federal Reserve System. 1943. *Banking and Monetary Statistics.* Washington, D.C.

Brunner, K., and Meltzer, A. H. 1968. "What Did We Learn from the Monetary Experience of the United States in the Great Depression?" *Canadian Journal of Economics* 1 (May): 334–48.

———. 1964. "The Federal Reserve's Attachment to the Free Reserves Concept." Subcommittee on Domestic Finance, Committee on Banking and Currency. Washington: United States House of Representatives. 88th Congress, 2nd Session.

Burgess, W. R. 1946. *The Reserve Banks and the Money Market*, revised ed. New York: Harper and Brothers.

Calomiris, C. W. 1990. "Is Deposit Insurance Necessary? A Historical Perspective." *Journal of Economic History* 50 (June): 283–95.

Chandler, L. V. 1958. *Benjamin Strong, Central Banker.* Washington: Brookings Institution.

———. 1971. *American Monetary Policy 1928–1941.* New York: Harper and Row.

Clarke, S. V. O. 1967. *Central Bank Cooperation: 1924–31.* New York: Federal Reserve Bank of New York.

Dutkowsky, D. 1984. "The Demand for Borrowed Reserves: A Switching Regression Model." *Journal of Finance* 39 (June): 407–24.

Dutkowsky, D., and Foote, W. 1985. "Switching, Aggregation, and the Demand for Borrowed Reserves." *Review of Economics and Statistics* 67 (May): 331–35.

Eichengreen, B. 1984. "Central Bank Cooperation under the Interwar Gold Standard." *Explorations in Economic History* 21 (January): 64–87.

Eichengreen, B., Watson, M. W., and Grossman, R. S. 1985. "Bank Rate Policy Under the Interwar Gold Standard: A Dynamic Probit Model." *Economic Journal* 95 (September): 725–45.

120

Epstein, G., and Ferguson, T. 1984. "Monetary Policy, Loan Liquidation, and Industrial Conflict: The Federal Reserve and the Open-Market Operations of 1932." *Journal of Economic History* 44 (December): 957–83.

Federal Reserve Board. *Annual Report* (various issues).

Federal Reserve Board. *Bulletin* (various issues).

Field, A. J. 1984a. "Asset Exchanges and the Transactions Demand for Money." *American Economic Review* 74 (March): 43–59.

1984b. "A New Interpretation of the Onset of the Great Depression." *Journal of Economic History* 64 (June): 489–98.

Friedman, M., and Schwartz, A. J. 1963. *A Monetary History of the United States, 1867–1960.* New York: National Bureau of Economic Research.

Gendreau, B. C. 1990. "Federal Reserve Credit Policy in the Great Depression." Unpublished manuscript.

Goldenweiser, E. A. 1951. *American Monetary Policy.* New York: McGraw-Hill.

Goldfeld, S. M. 1966. *Commercial Bank Behavior and Economic Activity.* Amsterdam: North-Holland.

Goldfield, S. M., and Kane, E. J. 1966. "The Determinants of Member Bank Borrowing: An Econometric Study." *Journal of Finance* 21 (September): 499–514.

Gorton, G. 1985. "Clearinghouses and the Origin of Central Banking in the United States." *Journal of Economic History* 45 (June): 277–83.

Hamilton, J. D. 1987. "Monetary Factors in the Great Depression." *Journal of Monetary Economics* 19 (March): 145–69.

Harris, S. E. 1933. *Twenty Years of Federal Reserve Policy.* 2 vols. Cambridge: Harvard University Press.

Hayek, F. A. 1984 [1932]. "The Fate of the Gold Standard." in Money, Capital and Fluctuations, Early Essays of F. A. Hayek, edited by R. McCloughy. London: Routledge and Kegan Paul.

Hodgman, D. 1961. "Member Bank Borrowing: A Comment." *Journal of Finance* 16:90–93.

Johnston, J. 1984. *Econometric Methods*, 3rd ed. New York: McGraw Hill.

Kindleberger, C. P. 1986. *The World in Depression 1929–1939.* 2nd ed. Berkeley: University of California Press.

1988. "The Financial Crises of the 1930s and the 1980s: Similarities and Differences." *Kyklos* 41:171–86.

Lucia, J. L. 1985. "The Failure of the Bank of United States: A Reappraisel." *Explorations in Economic History* 22:402–16.

Mayer, T., Duesenberry, J. S. and Aliber, R. Z. 1987. *Money, Banking, and the Economy.* 3rd ed. New York: W. W. Norton.

Meigs, A. J. 1962. *Free Reserves and the Money Supply.* Chicago: University of Chicago Press.

Meltzer, A. H. 1976. "Monetary and Other Explanations of the Start of the Great Depression." *Journal of Monetary Economics* 2 (November): 455–71.

Miron, J. A. 1986. "Financial Panics, the Seasonality of the Nominal Interest Rate, and the Founding of the Fed." *American Economic Review* 76 (March): 124–40.

1988. "The Founding of the Fed and the Destabilization of the Post-1914 Economy." Cambridge, MA: National Bureau of Economic Research Working Paper No. 2701.

Riefler, W. 1930. *Money Rates and Money Markets in the United States.* New York: Harper and Brothers.

Schwartz, A. J. 1981. "Understanding 1929–1933." In *The Great Depression Revisited,* edited by Karl Brunner, pp. 5–48. Boston: Kluwer-Nihoff.

Temin, P. 1976. *Did Monetary Forces Cause the Great Depression?* New York: W. W. Norton.

1989. *Lessons from the Great Depression.* Cambridge, Mass.: The MIT Press.

Thornton, D. L. 1988. "The Borrowed-Reserves Operating Procedure: Theory and Evidence." *Review,* Federal Reserve Bank of St. Louis (January/February): 30–54.

Timberlake, R. H. 1978. *The Origins of Central Banking in the United States.* Cambridge: Harvard University Press.

1984. "The Central Banking Role of Clearinghouse Associations." *Journal of Money, Credit, and Banking* 16 (February): 1–15.

Toma, M. 1989. "The Policy Effectiveness of Open Market Operations in the 1920s." *Explorations in Economic History* 26 (January): 99–116.

Trescott, P. B. 1982. "Federal Reserve Policy in the Great Depression: A Counterfactual Assessment." *Explorations in Economic History* 19 (July): 211–20.

Turner, R. C. 1938. *Member Bank Borrowing.* Columbus: Ohio State University.

United States House of Representatives. 1926. *Stabilization.* Hearings Before the Committee on Banking and Currency. 69th Congress, 1st Session.

United States House of Representatives. 1935. *Banking Act of 1935.* Committee on Banking and Currency. 74th Congress, 1st Session.

United States Senate. 1931. *Operation of the National and Federal Reserve Banking Systems.* Committee on Banking and Currency. 71st Congress, 3rd Session.

1935. *Banking Act of 1935.* Committee on Banking and Currency. 74th Congress, 1st Session.

West, R. C. 1977. *Banking Reform and the Federal Reserve 1863–1923.* Ithaca: Cornell University Press.

Wheelock, D. C. 1987. "The Strategy and Consistency of Federal Reserve Monetary Policy, 1919–1933." Unpublished dissertation. University of Illinois at Urbana.

1989. "The Strategy, Effectiveness, and Consistency of Federal Reserve Monetary Policy 1924–1933." *Explorations in Economic History* 26 (October): 453–76.

1990a. "Interest Rate Seasonality, Financial Panics, and Federal Reserve Policy During the Great Depression." Center for Economic Research Working Paper no. 88-07. Department of Economics, University of Texas at Austin.

1990b. "Member Bank Borrowing and the Fed's Contractionary Monetary Policy During the Great Depression." *Journal of Money, Credit, and Banking* (November): 409–26.

White, E. N. 1983. *The Regulation and Reform of the American Banking System 1900–1929.* Princeton: Princeton University Press.

1984. "A Reinterpretation of the Banking Crisis of 1930." *Journal of Economic History* 44 (June): 119–38.

Wicker, E. 1965. "Federal Reserve Monetary Policy, 1922–33 A Reinterpretation." *Journal of Political Economy* 74 (August): 325–43.

1966a. *Federal Reserve Monetary Policy 1917–1933*. New York: Random House.

1966b. "A Reconsideration of Federal Reserve Policy during the 1920–1921 Depression." *Journal of Economic History* 26 (June): 223–38.

1969. "Brunner and Meltzer on Federal Reserve Monetary Policy During the Great Depression," *Canadian Journal of Economics* 2 (May): 318–21.

1980. "A Reconsideration of the Causes of the Banking Panic of 1930." *Journal of Economic History* 40 (September): 571–83.

1982. "Interest Rate and Expenditure Effects of the Banking Panic of 1930." *Explorations in Economic History* 19:432–45.

Index

For EU product safety concerns, contact us at Calle de José Abascal, 56–1°,
28003 Madrid, Spain or eugpsr@cambridge.org.

www.ingramcontent.com/pod-product-compliance
Ingram Content Group UK Ltd.
Pitfield, Milton Keynes, MK11 3LW, UK
UKHW040735250425
457623UK00033B/31